FOUNDATIONS OF MODERN PSYCHOLOGY SERIES

Richard S. Lazarus, *Editor*

SARNOFF A. MEDNICK

Associate Professor of Psychology, University of Michigan; author and researcher in the fields of conditioning and stimulus generalization, associative processes, learning, and abnormal thinking.

With the collaboration of HOWARD R. POLLIO
Assistant Professor of Psychology, University of Tennessee.

Learning

25014

PRENTICE-HALL, INC., Englewood Cliffs, New Jersey

LEARNING, Sarnoff A. Mednick

Second printing......August, 1964

PRENTICE-HALL FOUNDATIONS
OF MODERN PSYCHOLOGY SERIES

Richard S. Lazarus, *Editor*

PRENTICE-HALL INTERNATIONAL, INC., LONDON
PRENTICE-HALL OF AUSTRALIA, PTY., LTD., SYDNEY
PRENTICE-HALL OF CANADA, LTD., TORONTO
PRENTICE-HALL OF INDIA (PRIVATE) LTD., NEW DELHI
PRENTICE-HALL OF JAPAN, INC., TOKYO
PRENTICE-HALL DE MEXICO, S.A., MEXICO CITY

Designed by Harry Rinehart

C–52705(p), C–52707(c)

Foundations
of Modern Psychology
Series

The tremendous growth and vitality of psychology and its increasing fusion with the social and biological sciences demand a new approach to teaching at the introductory level. The basic course, geared as it usually is to a single text that tries to skim everything—that sacrifices depth for superficial breadth —is no longer adequate. Psychology has become too diverse for any one man, or a few men, to write about with complete authority. The alternative, a book that ignores many essential areas in order to present more comprehensively and effectively a particular aspect or view of psychology, is also insufficient. For in this solution, many key areas are simply not communicated to the student at all.

The Foundations of Modern Psychology is a new and different approach to the introductory course. The instructor is offered a series of short volumes, each a self-contained book on the special issues, methods, and content of a basic topic by a noted authority who is actively contributing to that particular field. And taken together, the volumes cover the full scope of psychological thought, research, and application.

The result is a series that offers the advantage of tremendous flexibility and scope. The teacher can choose the subjects he wants to emphasize and present them in the order he desires. And without necessarily sacrificing breadth, he can provide the student with a much fuller treatment of individual areas at the introductory level than is normally possible. If he does not have time to include all the volumes in his course, he can recommend the omitted ones as outside reading, thus covering the full range of psychological topics.

Psychologists are becoming increasingly aware of the importance of reaching the introductory student with high-quality, well-written, and stimulating material, material that highlights the continuing and exciting search for new knowledge. The Foundations of Modern Psychology Series is our attempt to place in the hands of instructors the best textbook tools for this purpose.

Preface

The first chapter of this book describes training a primitive flat worm to respond to a light with body contraction. To me, teaching this little beast to twitch on signal is still a bit of a miracle. It is, however, only a hint of the potential power given by the knowledge of the basic principles of learning. Through conditioning techniques we teach pigeons to play ping-pong or direct missiles; we control the temperature and blood flow in specific parts of the body. At the University of Michigan, in Dr. James Olds' laboratory, I recently "contacted" a single nerve cell in the brain of a living white rat and trained this *cell* to increase and then decrease its rate of firing. The field of learning and behavior, a young science, can begin to look forward to the day when its potential for control of human beings will become a social problem. It is not unimportant that citizens be informed in these matters.

The facts of learning are among the basic facts of behavior. For this reason learning principles have been applied in a variety of fields. Neurotic and psychotic behaviors have been productively studied as learning disturbances. In education, teaching machines are a direct product of operant conditioning principles; the teaching machine is likely to be an opening wedge in a rather belated application of learning principles to the field of education. In industrial and defense applications, principles of the learning of motor skills are crucial in the design of man-machine systems.

This list only begins to tap the surface of the topic. I recited the list both because I wish to emphasize the importance of the field and because with rare exception these applications are not mentioned again in this book. Instead the book contains a description of some of the salient basic facts we have gathered concerning the learning process. I have tried to take account of the most recent research, but have also made a conscious attempt to cite early work when possible. I would urge the introductory student to read this book in the sequence that it has been written. Chapters build on previous chapters. The early chapters provide a basic language and "feel" for learning research. These are then assumed in later chapters.

I owe much to Dr. Howard Pollio for his help in drafting materials for Chapters 3, 6, and 7 during the busy days at the University of Michigan just prior to my leaving for a year of research in Denmark. During my current absence from the United States he has carried the burden of procuring illustrations, proofreading, and preparing the index. Mr. Leo Hansen of Kommunehospitalet has been extremely generous in providing space and facilities for my work. My thanks also for the encouragement of my kind Danish friends.

Dr. Richard Lazarus and Dr. G. Robert Grice both provided me with highly useful criticisms of various drafts of the manuscript. Benton J. Underwood taught me most of what I know about science and about learning; his review of the first draft of this manuscript both encouraged me and, more importantly, set me straight on some matters he had not quite attended to while I was still a student. Miss Karin Winther Pedersen patiently and skillfully typed and retyped this manuscript.

Sarnoff A. Mednick

Contents

Some Examples
of Research on Learning

The planarian (*Dugesia dorotocephala*) is a primitive flatworm that tends to dwell on the underside of rocks in mildly stagnant, polluted water. In many ways the planarian, only three-quarters of an inch long, is an outstanding creature (see Figure 1-1). From the point of view of evolutionary development, however, it must be confessed that he has not come very far in complexity. Despite this considerable handicap, planaria can learn, as experiments have proved. The method used to induce them to do so is a good starting point for studying learning, since it involves one of the simplest types of learning psychologists investigate.

I

1

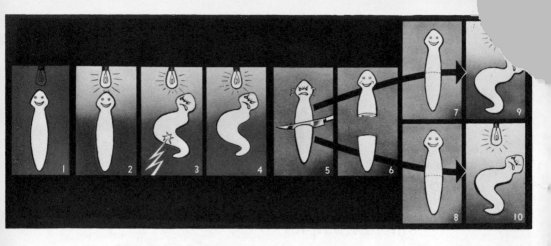

Figure 1-1.   In terms of evolution planaria are the earliest organisms to have developed a concentration of nerve fibers that could be called a "brain." Because of this, researchers have been interested in the planarian's ability to learn. The first four panels of this figure are discussed in the text. When a light and electric shock are paired, as in Panel 3, planaria eventually learn to respond to the light with contraction, the response they ordinarily give to the shock (as in Panel 4). If a planarian is cut into pieces each piece regenerates a complete organism. James V. McConnell, Allan L. Jacobson, and Daniel P. Kimble took planaria which had learned to contract to the light and cut them in half (Panels 5 and 6). They then allowed the halves to regenerate as in Panels 7 and 8. The question was: if each half was then tested with the light would any memory be shown? Would the head end show better memory than the tail end? As is illustrated in Panels 9 and 10 both heads and tails showed retention of the light—contraction association. What was of special interest is that there was no difference in the amount of retention exhibited in the head and tail ends. The intriguing question stemming from this research is, how does retention occur in the tail section? Some very recent evidence suggests that it is partially chemical in nature. (Courtesy Science et Vie.)

An experimenter can get a planarian to learn to make a certain *response,* a simple body contraction, whenever he turns on a 100-watt light bulb, located six inches above the planarian's head. We can assume that the flatworm learns this response to the light *stimulus* because when the lamp is first turned on, for three-second flashes, he takes little notice. But during training, in the last of the three seconds that the light remains on, he is regularly jolted with an electric shock delivered through the water. He need not learn his response to the shock; it is a reflexive body contraction. If the light and shock are presented together about 250 times the contraction response will reliably occur with only the light. Clearly, the humble planarian has learned to respond to the light he previously ignored.

Such a change in behavior as a result of experience is learning. In the remainder of this chapter we shall skim across the field that psychologists call learning, touching down periodically to illustrate a method or to introduce a theory. This brief survey of "learning psychology" is intended to give you quick glance at a map showing the whole of this area before leading you down the first side street.

Conditioning

The method of training used with the planarian is called *classical conditioning*. It consists of repeatedly pairing a neutral stimulus (in this case the light) with a stimulus (electric shock) which invariably elicits a response (contraction) until the neutral stimulus alone will elicit the response. It is based on a method of conditioning first systematically investigated by the Russian physiologist Ivan Pavlov. In later chapters we shall consider classical conditioning and the work of Pavlov in great detail, for despite its apparent simplicity classical conditioning has wide implications for human behavior. Psychologists were forced to use the modifier "classical" when a new kind of conditioning, *operant conditioning,* was first systematically studied and reported by B. F. Skinner in 1938. Although Skinner did most of his original work with white rats as laboratory subjects, his methods have found broad application.

To give you an idea of what this second sort of conditioning is, it might be best to start with an example, a project being conducted in an operant conditioning research laboratory in a mental hospital in Massachusetts. Experiments are carried on in specially constructed rooms that happen to be in the basement of the building. Dealing with very seriously disturbed patients, the experimenters have often found it quite difficult simply to get the patients to come down to the experiment rooms. An undergraduate from a nearby university, well versed in operant conditioning procedures, took it upon himself to attempt to bring a patient with a long-standing mental illness to one of these rooms. Illness had reduced this patient to an almost animal state. He had little or no control over defecation or urination; he would often bite individuals who came too close to him; he did not speak. Consequently, he was kept in virtual isolation.

In order to get him downstairs, the student used an operant conditioning technique called "shaping-up." In this method the experimenter continually rewards acts that come closer and closer to some ultimately desired behavior. Thus, the student waited for the first time the patient turned his head toward the door leading to the basement stairs. At this point he presented the patient with a small piece of candy which the latter quickly ate. (It had been previously determined that the patient liked candy.) Presently, the patient faced the door again, and again the student was there with a piece of candy. After a number of such incidents the patient simply stood facing the door. The candy acted as a *reward* for door-facing and increased the likelihood, or

Some Examples of Research on Learning

3

probability, of its occurrence. After this phase of training was completed, the student withheld the candy until the patient took a step. When the patient had received candy several times for taking steps, the student again withheld candy until he took steps in the direction of the basement stairs. After a number of days, during which there were many reversals and disappointments, the patient actually walked down the stairs, entered a basement room, and went through the experimental procedures. This was the first time in some years that the patient had behaved in such an organized manner.

This example of shaping-up illustrates the effectiveness of systematically administered reward, the most important feature of operant conditioning. The shaping-up method has recently been applied to education via teaching machines. The pupil is rewarded for progressing in small stages in acquiring the desired information.

Operant conditioning differs from classical conditioning in certain ways. For example, classical conditioning only applies in situations where a response is inevitable; in the planarian, for instance, contraction is an automatic reflex to electric shock. In operant conditioning, by contrast, the experimenter must patiently wait for the response to occur naturally before he can increase its probability with a reward. We shall discuss this and other differences and their implications in Chapter 3.

Maze Learning

We can analyze both classical and operant conditioning in terms of *stimuli, responses,* and *rewards.* In order to study these units as they combine in complex series, psychologists have devised a number of appropriate procedures. Among these the maze has been one of the most widely used with animals. The simplest form is the *T-maze* (Figure 1-2) wherein an animal must choose between a left or right turn at the point of choice. If he chooses correctly he is rewarded with food in the goal box. The set-up may be further complicated by adding more points of choice, as in the multiple T-maze (Figure 1-3).

D. A. MacFarlane used a maze in a clever experiment designed to test a theory that had been advanced by John B. Watson. Watson had suggested that what a rat learns in running to the goal box of a maze is not a map of the maze, but simply a series of mechanical leg and body movements involved in turning left or right. MacFarlane reasoned that if a rat learns to negotiate the maze with one series of movements and is later required to use another set of movements, then, according to Watson, there would be disruption in the rat's ability to traverse the maze. MacFarlane tested this theory by filling a maze with water to a depth of eight inches. The rats he used had to swim to find the goal box. They did. (Rats swim quite well.) Next, without changing the appearance of the structure, MacFarlane put a floor in the entire maze one inch

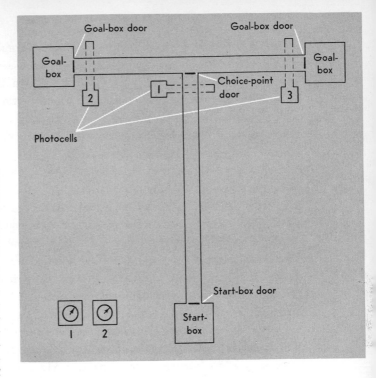

Figure 1-2.   Drawing of a simple T-maze. Rat is placed in the starting box and when he is facing forward, the door is raised. The door is closed to prevent the animal from retracing its steps. When the animal crosses photocell 1, the first clock is stopped, giving a measure of running time from the opening of the start box door to reaching the choice point. When the animal reaches either photocell 2 or 3, clock 2 is stopped, giving a measure of the total time from opening the start box door to reaching one of the goal boxes. Once the rat enters the goal box the door is dropped to detain him there until he consumes the reward. (From D.J. Lewis, Scientific principles of psychology. *Englewood Cliffs, N.J.: Prentice-Hall, 1963.)*

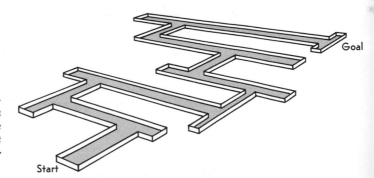

Figure 1-3.   A schematic representation of a multiple T-maze. The door here shown is at the entrance; interior doors are not shown.

beneath the surface of the water. Now the rats had to wade. Since movements in swimming and wading are quite different, Watson would have predicted a great confusion as a result of this change. As a matter of fact, almost no confusion occurred. The rats waded through the maze with great aplomb and few errors, thereby casting considerable doubt on the Watsonian interpretation. It seems clear that rats learn something more than a series of body movements when they learn to traverse a maze.

Mazes have also been utilized to study how humans learn a series of responses. The original model for such mazes was the complex arrangement of hedges that is found at Hampton Court Palace, in England. But since such a magnificent set of hedges may take up to eight years to grow, psychologists have developed more conventient devices such as table models that simply require a subject to find his way by tracing a path with his finger.

Verbal Learning

Besides mazes, psychologists also use various forms of verbal tasks in studying learning. In one method, called *serial verbal learning,* they ask people to learn to connect a series of words in order to evaluate the factors affecting their ability to learn serial tasks. One of the pioneers in verbal learning research, Hermann Ebbinghaus, wished to study the process of verbal learning without the troublesome contaminating effects of the previous experience people have with words. To circumvent this problem he devised a new verbal unit that could not have been previously experienced—the *nonsense syllable.* Nonsense syllables are relatively meaningless three-letter combinations composed of a vowel flanked by two consonants, for example, XAD. Ebbinghaus' idea of avoiding the effect of old habits by using novel nonsense syllables was a brilliant experimental innovation, but it proved to be only partially successful. For it was soon discovered that even nonsense syllables are affected by previous experience. For example, SYN is close enough to a popular English word to function in learning experiments almost the same way as does the real three-letter word. This property of nonsense syllables is called *meaningfulness;* lists of nonsense syllables have been rated for their meaningfulness by determining how regularly these syllables tend to suggest associated words or ideas to groups of judges.

John A. McGeoch conducted an experiment to determine what effect this property has on the ease of learning nonsense syllables. He arranged groups

TABLE 1

The Amount of Recall as a Function of Meaningfulness of Learned Material

Material	*Mean Number in a List of Ten*
3-letter words	9.11
High-meaningful nonsense syllables	7.35
Medium-meaningful nonsense syllables	6.41
Low-meaningful nonsense syllables	5.09

From McGeoch, J.A. *J. genet. Psychol.,* 1930, 37, 425.

of ten nonsense syllables each into three lists that differed in their meaning-fulness (very high, medium, very low). In addition, he used a fourth list of real three-letter words. He allowed subjects to study each list and then asked them to recall as many items as they could. The types of lists and the average number of items recalled from each appear in Table 1. As you can see, people recalled more and more items in a list as the meaningfulness increased.

Mediation

Many other studies using a variety of materials have confirmed these results: The more meaningful the material the faster people can learn it. One possible interpretation of this finding, although by no means the only possible interpretation, suggests that meaningful items facilitate learning largely because they have appeared in many contexts and have a variety of associations that can help bridge the gaps among them. The learner may not even be aware of this bridging process. For example, adopting the method of a study by Wallace Russell and Lowell Storms, I taught college students to associate a word to a nonsense syllable and then tested them to see whether this prior experience could serve as a bridge in learning a different but related word in association with the same nonsense syllable. Learning to associate a pair of verbal units is called, ap-propriately enough, *paired-associate learning*. In this study subjects learned to associate a list of pairs containing XAD—doctor and then were tested by having to learn a list of pairs containing XAD—Indian chief. Because they had learned the pair XAD—doctor and had previously learned the phrase "doctor, lawyer, Indian chief," the words doctor and lawyer apparently served as a bridge to learning the pair XAD—Indian chief. Furthermore, the latter pair was learned more quickly than other pairs that lacked such a bridging se-quence. It is noteworthy that in such experiments subjects are almost never able to report any of the bridges, or indeed anything at all concerning this process. This suggests that bridging can occur outside of awareness, or uncon-sciously. As might be expected, "aware" learners benefit the most from bridg-ing. This type of bridging in learning is called *mediation*.

As promised we have introduced some examples of the way learning is studied.

1. Classical conditioning in the planarian.
2. Operant conditioning of a mental patient.
3. Maze learning in the rat.
4. Nonsense-syllable verbal learning.
5. Paired-associate verbal learning and mediation.

We shall now continue this survey by observing how one very important variable, motivation, affects learning.

Learning is a sensitive process that is easily affected by changes in the learner or in the environment. In the pages that immediately follow we shall present some examples of experiments that test the effect of variations in motivation. We shall consider three aspects of motivation.

1. As an *energizer* of behavior (a hungry rat runs very quickly to find a goal box containing food).

2. As an *internal sensation* to which an animal may learn to behave *selectively* (we eat when hungry and drink when thirsty).

3. As a state of imbalance that can be rectified, thus resulting in a condition known as *reward* or *reinforcement* (if the state of imbalance is one of hunger, the appropriate rectifier would be food).

Motivation as an Energizer

Perhaps we can most clearly demonstrate the role of motivation as an energizer of behavior by pointing up the difference between learning and performance. The crucial differentiating element is that you can *see* performance. To "see" learning you would have to cut subjects open somehow and look in the right place, at the right time, in the right way. At our present state of technological advancement this is impossible, and besides, doing so would spoil subjects for other things. Let us take an example. Say we place a hungry rat that has been deprived of food for 24 hours in a T-maze with a one-gram chunk of rat food in the left arm of the maze. After a number of successful trials, following each of which he is put back in the starting box and new food is placed in the goal box, the rat will run quickly and unhesitatingly to the goal box, showing that he must have learned where the food is located and how to get there. After about 15 trials, however, the rat will become increasingly reluctant to leave the starting box. He may simply find himself a comfortable corner and go to sleep. The reason is simple; after 15 such trials he will have eaten 15 grams of food, which is just about the rat equivalent of a five-course dinner.

Why isn't the rat still performing? The answer is that his hunger has been satisfied and he is no longer motivated to perform. His level of learning has not diminished, though. If he wakes up hungry he will quickly demonstrate his ability to run the maze with speed and without error. It is clear that we need *both* learning and motivation for performance. Motivation without learning will simply result in random activity; learning without motivation will simply result in inactivity, such as sleep.

One of the most influential motives in civilized society is anxiety. You

yourself may not have experienced serious hunger, thirst, or oxygen deprivation recently, but you probably have experienced some anxiety—consider
the time of your last final exam. Anxiety as well as hunger can motivate
learning in animals and men. If we were to electrify the floor of the maze,
we would quickly see the massive energizing effect a little appropriately administered "motivation" has on our sleeping rat. Further, if we provided an
island of safety from shock in one arm of the maze, the rat would soon learn to
run there to escape.

Motivation as a Cue

After a long walk in the
hot sun we begin to experience dryness in throat and mouth; we dub these
feelings thirst. When we feel them we look for a drink. Our seeking demonstrates again the energizing property of motives. That we would bypass dry,
salted popcorn for a tall glass of beer points up the association with specific
motives (thirst) of individual internal stimulus patterns (dry mouth and
throat) that direct behavior. Fear too can have such an effect. Mark May
conducted an intricate experiment showing how fear can produce an internal
stimulus pattern to which a rat can learn a specific response, just as though the
stimulus were external, such as a light. The experiment was conducted in
three stages, as follows:

1. May placed rats into compartment A of a two-compartment box; the units
were separated by a low hurdle. He then electrified the floor of compartment A.
The rats showed all the usual signs of fear including urination, defecation, and
crouching. They soon learned, however, to jump the hurdle into the safety of
compartment B to escape the shock. Note that the shock evoked fear, which was
one of the stimuli that led to jumping the hurdle.
2. The hurdle was removed and the rats were trapped in a covered cage in the
center of the box so that they could not jump. He then shocked them and at the
same time sounded a buzzer. They presumably learned to fear the buzzer. Now,
May reasoned, the buzzer should provoke fear in the rat. The fear should produce
certain stimuli. And the rat should have learned that when these fear stimuli are
present he should jump the hurdle to escape.
3. To test this assumption, May replaced the hurdle in the center of the box,
placed the rats one at a time in compartment A and sounded the buzzer. Sure
enough, the rats immediately jumped the hurdle. The sequence might read:
buzzer → internal fear stimuli → jump.

"But wait," the skeptic might say, "of course the rats jumped the hurdle;
they were startled and were merely energized into doing something and so
they jumped. It is crucial to your argument to demonstrate that the rats
actually experience the fear stimuli in response to the buzzer. Suppose you
take some rats and train them to jump the hurdle to escape just as May did
(Step 1). Then (Step 2) trap the rats in the center of the box as before (with

the hurdle removed), but instead of sounding the buzzer and shocking them at the same time, give them the same number of shocks as the other rats, and sound the buzzer as often but don't present the buzzer and shock at the same time. Now, because the buzzer and shock have not been presented together, the buzzer should not cause fear in the rat. May would then predict that in the third stage, the second group would not jump the hurdle when the buzzer was sounded. If they do jump the hurdle it is clear they do so because it is the only thing they can do, not because the buzzer brings on the fear stimuli to which the jumping response was trained."

As a matter of fact, in anticipation of such criticism, May *did* train a control group of rats in the second manner. In comparison to his experimental group, however, very few of the control group jumped the hurdle when the buzzer was sounded. Clearly then, the buzzer elicited in the rats distinct fear stimuli in response to which they had learned to jump.

Like the rats, we all have learned to make certain responses when we are anxious or fearful. When some people feel anxious, they nervously go about straightening up tie or desk; when an adolescent feels anxious, the classic response is to look down at the floor and go through some intricate foot shuffling. It has been suggested that unusual and aberrant thinking is actually a response a mentally ill person has learned to make when he feels fearful. The "crazy" thinking allows him to escape from current reality and consequently serves to reduce his fear.

Motivation as a Need To Be Satisfied

In the operant conditioning of the schizophrenic patient described above, the student waited for the desired behavior to occur and then presented the patient with candy. When the rat jumped the hurdle, he escaped the electric shock. When the hungry rat went down the left arm of the T-maze he received one gram of rat food. Each act was concluded with some favorable experience; such an experience is usually called a *reward* or *reinforcement*. As a rule, behavior that leads to reinforcement or regularly precedes reinforcement, tends to recur. In fact some psychologists turn the emphasis around and simply *define* reinforcement as anything that increases the probability of behavior that systematically precedes it.

One theorist, Clark Hull, maintains that reinforcement is brought about by the reduction of a need. For instance, when a rat eats the food in the left arm of the T-maze, his hunger is reduced. This approach has raised a number of questions. One is: When does the reinforcement involved in eating actually occur? There are several possible ways of asking this question.

1. Is it when the food first enters the organism's mouth?
2. Is it when the food is on its way to the stomach?
3. Is it only when the food reaches the stomach?
4. Is it when the "food" enters the blood stream?
5. Is it when the "food" is utilized by a body cell?

There have been a number of attempts to achieve answers to these questions. Let us examine one of them. In an effort to test the fourth choice, H. W. Coppock and Randall M. Chambers strapped a hungry rat to a board and, by observing him carefully, determined which way he preferred to turn his head (rats have definite individual preferences in this regard). They then implanted a needle into the hungry rat's caudal vein so that they could, at will, inject a given amount of sugar solution directly into his blood stream. They thus "fed" him a little sugar solution every time he turned his head to his nonpreferred side. If this type of "feeding" could serve as a reinforcement, the rat should soon learn to change the direction of his head-turning preference. Coppock and Chambers reported that through this injection they did indeed alter the rat's preference. A control group of hungry rats were treated identically, except that they were "fed" with a salt solution. These animals did not learn to turn their heads in the nonpreferred direction. Clearly it was the motivation-reducing property of the sugar solution that was crucial rather than simply the addition of some liquid to the blood.

LEARNING AND HIGHER MENTAL PROCESSES

In the foregoing examples of research relatively low-level instances of learning have been emphasized. In this section something shall be done to correct this unbalanced picture. Perhaps I can most appropriately begin by describing some of the research of a man whose work was aimed at correcting this imbalance for psychology as a whole.

From an island off the coast of Africa, Wolfgang Köhler reported a series of experiments that were aimed at challenging simplistic explanations in psychology. Detained during World War I on this island, which had a native group of chimpanzees, Köhler took the opportunity to study "The Mentality of Apes" (the title of his book). Köhler's work was, in part, an attempt to refute earlier experiments by Edward L. Thorndike which suggested that animals are planless, generating merely random responses when confronted with a problem. In this view, they only "solve" a problem when some trial-and-error behavior gains in strength as a result of being followed by reinforcement. Köhler's observations led him to question this view. He suggested that if the relevant objects were clearly presented, animals could solve problems insightfully by seeing the relationships between the items. Once an animal had *insight* it would pass from random behavior to perfect performance in one trial, not improve gradually, reinforcement by reinforcement.

Why did Köhler come to this conclusion? In one experiment he placed a chimpanzee and a stick in a cage. Outside the cage was a banana. The chimp first tried to grasp the banana with his hand but it was out of reach. Eventually he picked up the stick and played with it. At one point he suddenly rushed to the bars with the stick, reached out and swept in his prize. The change in behavior was sudden and complete as though insight had occurred, not slow and gradual.

On hearing of this work Pavlov objected, suggesting that Köhler had not controlled the past conditioning history of the chimpanzees. He judged that sudden insight without this prior conditioning was impossible. There is some recent evidence which suggests that Pavlov may have been right. Herbert G. Birch placed a laboratory-raised chimpanzee in a cage with food outside it beyond his reach. A rake of sorts was in perfect position for drawing in the food. Only one of six chimps seemed to arrive at a truly "insightful" solution in this pat situation. As it turned out this chimp had had previous experience along these lines. In an attempt to generate relevant conditioning as suggested by Pavlov, Birch allowed the chimps free play for some time with sticks. After this play experience the chimps very quickly gave insightful solutions to the rake problem. It seemed that insight in this situation depended in large part on the use of previously learned habits and associations.

An instructive analogy may be drawn between these insight experiments with animals and experiments on problem solving with human beings. Norman R.F. Maier has been responsible for devising a number of ingenious methods for studying how human adults attack problems. One of these is depicted in Figure 1-4. In this technique, a subject is asked to tie two ropes together; he may use anything in the room. There are a number of solutions possible; the difficulty is that while holding one rope he normally cannot reach the other. An elegant solution consists of tying pliers, which are present, to the end of one rope and setting the rope swinging. By catching it while holding the second rope the ropes may be knotted. In a variation on this method, Abe J. Judson, Charles N. Cofer, and Sidney Gelfand attempted to provide subjects with associations that could be used to facilitate insight. They preceded the subjects' experience of the two-string problem with some paired-associate learning. For some subjects one of the stimulus words in the list was "rope" and its response was "swing"; other subjects learned to respond to "rope" with "hemp." The individuals with the relevant previous training (rope—swing) were more likely to arrive at the "swinging" solution. These

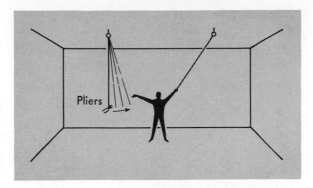

Figure 1-4.   The two-rope problem. The object is to join the ropes. One solution is to tie pliers to the end of one of the ropes and to set it swinging.

experiments suggest the role previous learning plays in higher mental processes. It is clear that certain fundamental habits and associations are crucial. The availability of these associations determine how easily higher mental processes such as problem-solving are carried on.

In presenting this research sampler I have attempted to give you a feeling for the breadth of the material covered and the subjects studied by researchers in the field of learning. In the following chapter we shall attempt to step back from these specific instances and descriptions of research and attempt to point out some of the underlying similarities in terms of common elements. We shall also get a picture of how a research problem in learning is planned and designed and how it is carried through to the final results.

The Language
and Methods of Learning

In Chapter 1 the survey covered a wide span—from conditioning of the planarian to human problem solving. You may wonder about the relationship between these extremes. Is there a continuum in learning from simple creatures to man? Although we can hardly imagine presenting complex problems to planaria, we do know that it is quite simple to condition responses in human beings. Also, the basic laws of conditioning seem the same as we move from one species to the other. In fact, we find that most of the fundamental laws of learning we derive from research on lower animals apply as well in research on man.

14

2

Then why do the research on lower organisms in the first place? There are many reasons. For one thing, some scientists who study learning just prefer to work with animals because animals are their major interest. For another, this type of work feeds on itself. There is a thick handbook concerned exclusively with psychological research on the white rat. So much is known about the behavior of this ubiquitous laboratory animal that an investigator studying simple learning by means of the rat has much of his background work already completed for him and can immediately focus on the specific problems engaging his interest.

In many cases learning researchers use dogs or rats as subjects where it is immoral, illegal, or simply inconvenient to use people. When the effect of acute operative damage to an area of the cortex is being studied, or the effect of being raised from birth in a specific restricted environment, animal work is the only moral and legal recourse. In Birch's experiment with chimpanzees and a rake we saw the advantage of observing an animal with a relatively controlled history of conditioning and learning. As you will recall, one of the six chimpanzees solved the problem on the first try. Birch notes that this chimpanzee was the only one that had had extensive experience in handling sticks in his pre-experimental daily life. In an experiment that stretches over days and weeks it is often crucial to strictly control the extra-experimental experiences of the subject; so animals in cages win out once again.

There is perhaps one more reason for the use of lower animals in learning research. Like all other sciences psychology grew from philosophy. The philosophical method of studying man consisted in the main of intuitive and searching self-explorations and thoughtful consideration of the behavior of others. Self-consciously building a *science,* certain psychologists in the first quarter of this century aggressively rejected any attempt to study such unmeasurable and secret things as thoughts. They wished to study tangible events that could be seen in the plain light of day and measured. Thoughts are not as tangible or as easily measured as a rat's speed in running a maze. In addition, when we put a man into a simple learning situation involving a voluntary response such as an arm movement, he is always thinking. These thoughts help determine his behavior. They are unmeasurable and constitute an unknown quantity in the experiment. If the rat is thinking, at least he cannot embarass us by telling us about it. These considerations led psychologists studying learning at the beginning of the century to work with animals. Since then, however, we have devised methods for the scientific study of the thinking itself.

One more point: If we wish to know how a man learned an arm movement before he could "think" about it, we must study organisms that do not already possess complex symbolic habits. For this purpose investigators turned to young children and lower animals.

Now, for a caution: We can never blindly assume that findings from animal research apply to human beings. Any specific research findings using animals must first be checked out with people. Where such findings cannot be checked on human beings because of the danger or discomfort of the procedures, generalization must be restricted since it will be based on indirect evidence. Why this concern with generalizing from animal research to humans? One of the things that scientists treasure most in their research and theory is elegance. One of the important components of elegance is parsimony. Parsimony is a rule of science which maintains that the world and its actions should be explained in the fewest possible number of laws. Clearly, if we can explain the behavior of both animals and men with the same set of laws, we are being parsimonious.

WHAT IS LEARNING?

Examples of Unlearned Behavior

Almost all adult human behavior is learned. Some behavior is reflexive or instinctive; we breathe, our heart pumps; our cells apparently teem with activity; our knees jerk. All of this behavior takes place without the benefit of learning. As we move down through lower animals, reflexes and instincts account for more and more of their behavior. There is sometimes a danger that a learning psychologist will ascribe to past learning some complex behavior that is actually instinctive. Take the baby duck. Ducklings characteristically tend to follow their mothers. It would be rather easy for the learning psychologist to explain this behavior from his armchair. The duckling follows the mother because it is often reinforced for doing so. It has, however, been demonstrated that this behavior is instinctive, occurring without any learning. At a certain crucial time, some hours after emerging from their shells, newborn ducklings can be induced to waddle after anything from a football to an experimenter that is moving nearby. The induction is accomplished by simply exposing the ducklings to the moving objects. They will continue to follow these objects from then on. This behavior, called *imprinting*, is not learned. Ethologists, who study comparative behavior, have observed even more complex unlearned behaviors. Let us examine one in some detail.

The subject of this examination is the stickleback, a relatively unobtrusive fresh water fish whose name derives from the bony spines that extend from its back. We mention the fish here because of its remarkable behavior patterns for courtship, mating, and defense. The male begins his courtship by

constructing an underwater nest. In order to make this nest into a home, the male stickleback must attract a suitable female. He approaches female fish only if they are receptive; female sticklebacks who are receptive advertise their condition by exhibiting a swollen abdomen. The male, in turn, communicates his interest by developing a red underbelly and by performing an intricate zig-zag dance. During this courtship period, the male stickleback defends the nest against other sexually active males, who are easily recognized by their red undersides. No red underbelly, no attack.

A series of experiments has shown that the occurrence of these complicated acts depends on specific stimuli in the environment of the stickleback. Thus, a mature male will make a sexual approach to a dummy fish, but only if the dummy has a swelling in the area of the abdomen (see Figure 2-1). The dummy need not resemble the female stickleback much; about all it needs is the abdominal swelling. Similarly, the sexually mature male will attack dummies that bear little resemblance to other sticklebacks, provided they have red underbellies.

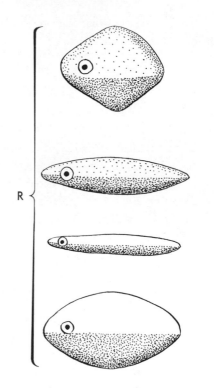

Figure 2-1. Dummies used to induce fighting in male sticklebacks. When a faithful model lacked the red underbelly there was no attack. The models labelled R, which have red under-bellies, all provoked fighting. (From V.G. Dethier and Eliot Stellar, Animal Behavior, 2nd ed. Englewood Cliffs, N.J.: Prentice-Hall, 1964.)

All this highly complex social behavior is carried off successfully even though a stickleback need never have learned it, or seen other sticklebacks behaving in such a manner. This intricate behavior pattern is built into sticklebacks when they are hatched. All that is necessary to elicit it is the occurrence of the *releasing stimulus*—the red belly or the swollen abdomen. Given the releasing stimulus, the response sequence is a foregone conclusion.

A Definition of Learning

We have devoted some space to stating what learning is not. What is it then? Learning has a number of defining characteristics.

1. *It results in a change in behavior.* We note a change in the planarian's response to the light. Now when it is presented the animal contracts.

2. *It comes about as a result of practice.* This characteristic eliminates sources of change such as illness and maturation. Recall the potent effects of motivation on behavior mentioned in Chapter 1. Changes in behavior caused by such variables are not considered learned.

3. They are not considered learned because they are temporary changes. *Learning, though, is a relatively permanent change.* After a rat wakes up from his nap he still remembers the path to the food. Even if you have not been on a bicycle for years, in just a few minutes' practice you can be quite proficient again. Continued practice at a well-learned task, however, might result in fatigue and poor performance. This change in behavior as a result of practice would not be considered learning since it is not permanent. A little rest will bring the performance up to par again.

4. *Learning is not directly observable.* We distinguished between learning and performance in Chapter 1. Learning is only one of the many variables influencing performance. Nevertheless, the only way to study learning is through some observable behavior. In research we often try to subtract the effects of all irrelevant variables by the use of a *control group*. If we are studying the effect of amount of *work* on speed of learning a maze, we might study rats with high hunger motivation running in a maze with a heavy load strapped to their backs. Despite the complicating effects introduced by the high motivation, we need it in order to get the rats to run in the maze. For a control group we may study a group of litter-mates running in the maze with identical hunger motivation but with only a pack of balsa wood on their backs. When we subtract the balsa-wood-group's results from the heavy-pack-group's results, we must ascribe any difference in maze performance to the effect of the heavy load since otherwise the groups are identical. May we now say we have observed differences in learning? No! These are only differences in performance. If we want to study pure learning differences we must now test both groups of rats in the maze either without any packs or with both groups wearing identical heavy or light packs (we would probably split our original groups and try all three). If we now find no differences in maze-running ability, then we can deduce that although amount of work has an effect on performance, it has no effect on learning.

We have already pointed out that we cannot actually observe learning; we see only what precedes performance, the performance itself, and the consequences of performance. Before proceeding to the complexities of this process it might be worthwhile to pause to define some words related to these three observable events.

What Precedes Performance

What precedes an act we usually call a *stimulus*. Stimuli can be as arresting and complex as the activities of an Egyptian belly dancer or as innately boring and simple as a pure tone of moderate frequency and intensity. The buzzer in May's hurdle-jumping experiment was a stimulus; however, so too was the complex of feelings associated with fear. This latter type of stimulus grows from impulses originating inside the organism and consequently is usually called an *internal stimulus*. You could argue that, technically, all stimuli are internal since they are not effective until they stimulate a sensory organ, such as the retina of the eye, and at that point they are quite "internal." Still, pragmatically it is useful to distinguish stimuli that clearly originate outside an organism from those that are within. Feelings of being thirsty or hungry are internal stimuli; *proprioceptive* is the special name applied to internal stimuli resulting from muscle movement. We are usually unaware of most of the internal stimulation that regulates our behavior. Did you realize that you were breathing 15 minutes ago and that this breathing was producing internal stimuli?

We measure stimuli. We use foot-candles to measure the brightness of a light, pounds per square inch to measure the intensity of pressure of a touch, decibels to measure the loudness of a tone, volts and amperes to measure the intensity of a shock, and wavelength to measure the hue of a light. It is clear that some stimuli are harder to measure than others, say, rumblings from a stomach. If pushed, though, we can even measure the number and strength of stomach rumblings. When we move away from physical dimensions the method of measurement changes. We can easily measure the size of a nonsense syllable, but what about its meaningfulness? As we pointed out in Chapter 1, we estimate this by the number of words or ideas the syllables suggest to the judges. If we specify carefully the conditions of the judgments, such as the instructions given to the judges, we have a useful definition of the meaningfulness of nonsense syllables. Indeed, we *would* specify all these determinants of the measure of meaningfulness to promote clarity of communication. Since we clearly specify the operations involved, this type of definition is called an *operational definition*. We could define the meaningfulness of a nonsense syllable in nonoperational terms—for instance, the feeling of "wordness" that the nonsense syllable conveys. But since this statement does not tell us how to go out and measure or observe meaningfulness, it is not an operational definition. In a sense, once we have operationally defined meaningfulness, future usage of the word is often only an abbreviated way of restating the operations of measurement. The major purpose of operational definitions is to promote clarity of communication.

This important function of operational definitions is clearly brought out by a consideration of another type of variable that usually precedes performance—motivation. If we were content to describe our experimental subjects as simply highly motivated, or very hungry, or quite desirous, our communication would not be precise. But we can operationally define a very hungry rat as one that has been starved for a specified number of hours after having been permitted to eat his fill.

The Performance Itself

The second stage we call the *response*. A response can be as complex as trying to rub your stomach in a circular motion with your left hand while patting your head with your right, or as simple as a twitch of a muscle in your forehead. Responses can come in any sizes but when they get to be highly complex, such as turning on lights, closing the shades, and turning up the heat, we usually call them acts. Like stimuli, responses can be relatively overt (screaming at the top of your lungs) or relatively covert (sweating). Both of these responses are measurable. We measure the loudness of the scream in decibels. We measure the amount of sweating by passing a small and undetectable electric current through the skin; when a person sweats the current passes through the skin more easily. This change in current flow, which can be detected by instruments, is called the *galvanic skin response,* GSR (or sometimes the psycho-galvanic response, PGR).

A response almost inevitably becomes a stimulus. If you respond to a stimulus with fear, you may sense your heart rate increasing, your blood pressure rising, your extremities getting cold and sweaty, and your breathing growing shallow. If you pay attention when you turn this page you will notice that your arm movements produce proprioceptive stimuli. The fear and the arm movements are responses that produce stimuli, hence the term *response-produced stimuli.* Furthermore, we can learn responses to response-produced stimuli. A good example is the rat in the May study that learned to jump the barrier when he sensed the internal stimuli produced by the fear response to the buzzer.

If methods already exist, such as for meaningfulness of syllables or for loudness of tones, the measurement of stimuli in a laboratory is usually not difficult, since the experimenter is the one who originates the buzzer or the shock. He knows what is coming and can either measure it beforehand or prearrange conditions so that he records or measures it during the experiment. But problems of measurement occur even with stimuli. Take the case of operant conditioning of the mental patient by the college student. The latter did not know what stimuli preceded the response he was conditioning; he simply waited for the response and then reinforced it. It is clear that in some kinds of learning research the stimuli will be difficult (some think unnecessary) to specify.

But we almost always must measure the response. We turn on the shock in the T-maze and look to see whether the animal learns to run to the island of safety in the left arm of the maze. If our point is, say, to detect the difference in effect of two levels of shock, we must measure the response as precisely as possible in order to know what effects different levels of shock have had. There are several major types of measurement available. The simplest measure is merely a count of the number of times the "correct" response (turning left in the T-maze and reaching the island of safety) occurs in a given number of trials. Thus, we can say that under shock level A a rat made the correct response in eight of ten trials; under shock level B he made the correct response in only three out of ten trials. This measure is called the *frequency* of response. We can also measure the amount of time it takes a response to get underway. We could put an electric-eye device at the exit of the starting box and wire a clock to turn on when the electric shock begins and stop when the rat, in leaving the starting box, interrupts the photo-electric beam. We call this measure the *latency* of response. In addition, we could have another clock wired to start with the electric shock and to stop when the rat reaches the island of safety. This would record *speed of response,* or *response time*. On some trials the rat may turn right instead of left; this would be an *error*. We can also measure the percentage of mistakes that occur. The percentage of correct responses and the percentage of errors give you the same information except when the rat does not leave the starting box. We also want to know how "large" a response is. An experimenter once harnessed rats to a pulley-and-spring device that measured the force of the rats' pull. He then varied the rats' motivation and measured the resultant differences in strength of pull as each rat left the starting box of the maze. This measure is called the *amplitude* of the response. After conditioning we sometimes wish to know how strong the conditioned response is. In the case of the planarian we could continue to present the light but omit the electric shock; the strength of the conditioned habit would be reflected by the number of trials on which the animal continues to respond to the light alone.

In operant conditioning we often measure the *rate of response*. As the college student reinforced the mental patient with candy for facing the door to the stairway, the patient turned to face the door more and more regularly. In the first hour he faced the door "hardly at all"; in the second hour "a little bit"; in the third hour "fairly often"; finally he faced it "almost all the time." In short, the rate of the door-facing response increased. The rate of response is a particularly applicable measure in operant conditioning situations. Since there is often no specific stimulus, it is hard to say when a trial begins; it is sensible, therefore, to count the *number of responses per unit of time*.

When we study the learning of word lists, we often measure the number of repetitions of the list before learning is completed; the "criterion for learning" is arbitrarily set at some level such as two or three consecutive perfect trials of the entire list. This measure is usually called "trials to criterion."

A Consequence of Performance: Reward

Operationally defined, a reward is an event that immediately follows a response and increases the likelihood of that response. Here is a case where an operational definition must be tied down at both the stimulus end (an event) and the response end (increases the likelihood of that response). "Events" in Chapter 1 that were rewards were escape from shock and the morsel of food at the end of the maze. The responses that increased in likelihood were, respectively, jumping the hurdle and turning left in the T-maze.

Figure 2-2. This rat, with an electrode implanted in his brain, has been placed in a Skinner box where his bar-pressing responses can be manipulated by electrical stimulation of the "pleasure" center of the brain. (Courtesy of Dr. James Olds.)

With animals the rewards in experiments are usually chosen to reduce some physiological need. A male rat completing a maze finds, depending on what he has been deprived of, a receptive female, or some food, or some water, or escape from an electric shock. The Coppock and Chambers rat turns his head to the right and has some sugar solution injected into his caudal vein.

In the course of investigating the effect of direct electrical stimulation of the brain upon a rat's behavior, James F. Olds and Peter Milner accidentally discovered a novel way to deliver a reward. The electrical stimulation is provided by a minute electrode implanted in the brain (Figure 2-2). One day, unknown to the experimenters, the placement of the electrode in one historic rat was slightly off target. The experimenters noted that when the rat was placed in an open field and stimulated (there is no pain at all associated with such stimulation), he tended to return repeatedly to the spot where he had been stimulated.

More stimulation at that place caused him to spend more of his time there. Later we found that this same animal could be pulled to any spot in the maze by giving a small electrical stimulus *after* each response in the right direction. This was akin to playing the hot and cold game with a child. Each correct response brought electrical pulses which seemed to indicate to the animal that it was on the right track. (From J. Olds and P. Milner. Positive reinforcement produced by electrical stimulation of septal area and other regions of rat brain. *J. comp. physiol. Psychol.*, 1954, 47, 419–427.)

In effect, what Olds and Milner had discovered was a place in the brain that acted as a "pleasure," or reward, center. In any case, after stimulation, the preceding response increased in likelihood, which is our definition of a reward. They tested further and found that even if starved the animal would pass up food in order to receive electrical stimulation. The rat learned to run in a T-maze to receive the stimulation. When the rat was killed and its brain microscopically examined, it was found that the electrode was in a portion of the brain called the anterior commissure. In subsequent research, the investigators have discovered that only very circumscribed areas of the brain produce a "reward" effect. Some areas are quite neutral; some areas produce a "punishment" effect. Research on these matters is in its early stages, but even now it is exceptionally exciting for it promises to help us understand the mechanism of the reward effect.

THE IMPORTANCE OF REWARD

In our discussion of rewards we have emphasized animal research. This stress is quite reasonable, since in animal learning the rewards are tangible and easily identified. But what is the reward in the case of a college student learning a list of nonsense syllables? Those psychologists who judge reinforcement to be necessary for learning suggest that when the college student succeeds in learning successive parts of the nonsense syllable list, he is rewarded because he is mastering a task. Although this explanation is not unreasonable, it is not satisfactory, since there is no way to observe the reward directly.

Sensory Preconditioning

A second explanation is more parsimonious. It grows from a theory that rewards are not necessary for learning. In this view, all that is necessary for learning is that a stimulus and a response occur at approximately the same time; this association is called temporal contiguity, or just contiguity. The stimulus will then have the power to evoke that response. There is a type of conditioning experiment called *sensory preconditioning* in which such learning has been demonstrated.

Two stimuli, such as a light and a tone, are presented together (contiguously) for a number of trials. One of these, say the tone, is then used as a training stimulus and is paired with meat powder blown into a dog's mouth. The meat powder automatically causes saliva to flow. After a number of pairings, the tone alone will produce a salivary response. After this initial training, the second stimulus, the light, is presented. Sensory preconditioning is said to occur if the salivation now occurs in response to the light. The first demonstration of sensory preconditioning was provided by W.J. Brogden, who felt his experiments proved unreinforced learning to be possible.

The mechanism of this learning has been explained in terms of mediation, a process we first met in Chapter 1 in the context of verbal learning. When the tone and light are presented together, the dog attends to them. For example, he may turn his head to the light and prick up his ears to the tone. It is possible that in the first stage a connection is established between the stimulus of the light and the dog's response to the tone.

1. light → pricking up ears (to tone)

In the second stage the tone is presented with the meat powder and becomes a stimulus for the salivary response. When the tone sounds the dog pricks up his ears as usual. This response produces proprioceptive stimuli that impinge on the dog at the same time the meat powder is blown into his mouth. Consequently these proprioceptive stimuli also become stimuli capable of eliciting the conditioned salivary response.

2. tone → pricking up of ears → proprioceptive stimuli
   meat powder → salivation

Now when the light is presented in the third stage it should elicit the response of pricking up of the ears (learned in the first stage). This response will produce proprioceptive stimuli. Since in stage two these proprioceptive stimuli became stimuli for the salivary response, that response should occur now too.

3. A. light → pricking up of ears
   B. pricking up of ears → proprioceptive stimuli
   C. proprioceptive stimuli → salivation

Notice that in this explanation the association between the light stimulus and the response of pricking up of ears is learned as a function of the *contiguity* of the stimulus and the response without any apparent reward.

Designing and Conducting an Experiment
on Contiguity Learning

Although this is a reason-
able explanation of this experiment, it possesses the same fault as the "task-mastery" reinforcement explanation of the college student learning a list of syllables. It depends heavily on events that have not been observed. To overcome this limitation, Brogden decided to attempt to condition an *overt* response to an *overt* stimulus without the aid of reinforcement simply by having them occur contiguously. His stimulus was a 1000-cycle tone of moderate intensity; his response was cage rotation (see Figure 2-4). His subjects were 23 kittens, 60 days old. The kittens came from six different litters, each of which was divided as equally as possible into the experimental (11 kittens) and control groups (12 kittens). In this way, anything unusual about a litter would affect the control and experimental groups equally, and consequently any future differences between these groups could not be ascribed to litter differences. Before beginning conditioning, Brogden made sure that his tone did not evoke the cage-turning response. Finding that it did not, he started conditioning the experimental group. In conditioning he presented the tone at the same time as the kittens made the cage-turning response. He waited for the response to occur; as soon as it did he turned the tone on for four seconds. The response and the tone had now been paired contiguously. After each kitten in the experimental group had 30 such trials, he ran 20 trials testing for the effects of conditioning, sounding the tone for four seconds when the kittens were quiet and watching for a conditioned cage-turning response. A conditioned response was tabulated if the kitten made a cage-turning response while the tone was on. His 11 experimental kittens made a total of 38 cage-turning responses. In order to decide whether conditioning had taken place he needed his control group for comparison purposes. How did he treat the control group? He went through exactly the same procedure as for the experimental group; but he allowed the control kittens to make the 30 cage-turning responses without any presentation of the tone. When he tested them with 20 presentations of the test tone, the 12 control

Figure 2-3. Rotator conditioning apparatus used in the study of contiguous conditioning. (Courtesy W. J. Brogden.)

kittens made a total of only seven cage-turning responses. The experimental group had made over five times as many (38). This clearly indicated that the frequent contiguous occurrence of the tone and the response had been sufficient to establish an association between them.

Apparently all that is necessary for an association to develop between a stimulus and a response is that they occur together frequently. Reward does not seem to be necessary. When reward is used, however, conditioning proceeds far more rapidly and with greater vigor. But in conditioning with rewards, the originally neutral stimulus is almost always presented before the response occurs. Thus, the light preceding the shock to the planarian served as a sort of signal that the shock was coming. It is in the nature of Brogden's technique that during the conditioning phase the tone was always sounded just after the response began. This sort of time relationship is called *backward conditioning*. As we shall see in the next chapter this is one of the least effective conditioning procedures. Perhaps the weak effect of contiguity conditioning in this experiment is due to this inverted stimulus-response sequence.

This chapter has introduced you to the methods, language, and thinking of researchers in the field of learning. We are now ready for a detailed examination of one of the important, simple building blocks of learning, conditioning.

Simple Learning: Classical and Operant Conditioning

Most organisms, even human beings, have responses that will be elicited automatically by certain stimuli without any previous learning. Shine a light into the pupil of the eye, or bite into a hamburger and in both cases predictable responses occur. In the former case, the pupil contracts, in the latter, saliva flows in the mouth. Such unlearned responses to stimuli are called *reflexes*; their common property is that they occur without any prior learning.

Pavlov made extensive use of the salivary reflex in his pioneering study of the simplest kind of learning: the

3

establishment of a new connection between a stimulus and a response. In the course of a series of studies on gastric secretions in dogs, he observed that the sound of the approaching footsteps of the dogs' keeper was sufficient to produce the flow of saliva. What was remarkable was that the dogs salivated even though the food had not yet been put into their mouths. Pavlov decided to make a systematic study of this reaction, which he called a "psychic secretion." Rather than continue to work with the footsteps of the keeper as a stimulus to evoke psychic secretions, Pavlov turned to more easily produced and controlled stimuli. Thus, he trained the dogs to salivate to a tuning fork rather than to footsteps. The basic procedure he used is called *classical conditioning*; it is already familiar to us since we described the classical conditioning of the planarian in Chapter 1.

The Basic Experiment

Before the experiment began, each dog underwent a simple operation to expose the duct of a salivary gland. This enabled Pavlov to measure responses by the number of drops of saliva secreted. The first step in the experiment was to sound the tuning fork alone to be sure that it didn't elicit salivation *before* training. (All it usually elicited was a turning of the head and a cocking of the ears.) After this possibility was eliminated, the sound of a tuning fork was presented to a dog at about the same time that meat powder was blown into his mouth. This pairing of meat powder and sound was repeated a number of times. Then Pavlov ran a test trial; he presented the sound of the tuning fork without the meat powder, and waited to see whether salivation would occur. It did. He also found that the more often the sound had been paired with the meat powder, the more the dog salivated to the sound alone. Table 2 shows the number of drops of saliva produced as a function of the number of pairings.

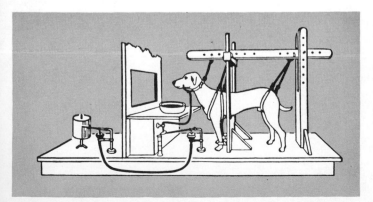

Figure 3-1. Pavlov's experimental arrangement. (From D.J. Lewis, Scientific principles of psychology. *Englewood Cliffs, N.J.: Prentice-Hall, 1963.*)

TABLE 2

Development of a Conditioned
Salivary Response in One Dog

Number of Presentations of Tuning Fork and Meat Powder	Drops of Saliva in 30 Seconds to Tuning Forks Alone
1	0
9	18
15	30
31	65
41	64
51	69

Taken from G.V. Anrep, *J. of Physiol.*, 1920.

The Language of Conditioning

Because Pavlov did so much of the original work in this area, it was he who coined the technical words to describe the procedure. He called the stimulus-response (S-R) connection acquired through this procedure the *conditional reflex;* by this he meant that the reflex was not innate but conditional on previous training. Somehow in the course of the translation of Pavlov's major book into English, the term *conditional* was improperly rendered as *conditioned,* and to the present day such an S-R connection is called a *conditioned reflex,* or, more generally, a *conditioned response* (CR). Pavlov called the meat powder an *unconditional stimulus,* and the reflexive salivation an *unconditional response.* A similar error in translation produced the current terms *unconditioned stimulus* (UCS) and *unconditioned response* (UCR). Pavlov called the tone the *conditional stimulus*—now, more usually, we say the *conditioned stimulus* (CS). The total procedure, called conditioning, is presented diagrammatically in Figure 3-2.

It is probably worthwhile to review these abbreviations for we shall use them extensively throughout the rest of the book:

CS (conditioned stimulus). In the Figure it was the tuning fork, which served as a signal for the meat powder which was the

UCS (unconditioned stimulus). This is a stimulus that can elicit a reflex response, salivation, termed the

UCR (unconditioned response). In conditioning this response becomes attached to the CS and is then called

CR (conditioned response).

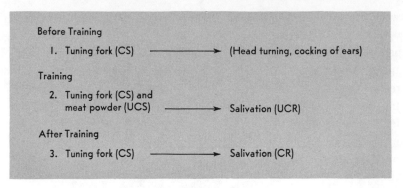

Figure 3-2.   A schematic diagram of the procedure for conditioning.

As you can see, before training, the sound (CS) has no tendency to produce salivation. It is only after the specific pairing of the sound with food (UCS) that the CS comes to evoke a reaction similar to the original UCR, namely the CR. In general, the study of conditioning consists of discovering the relationships that exist among these components. In Table 2 you saw the relationship between the number of pairings of the CS (sound) and the UCS (meat powder) and the amount of CR (salivation) evoked by the CS alone. There is a vast research literature in conditioning. We shall examine four questions considered in these writings.

1. What types of reflex responses may be made conditional to the presentation of a stimulus? Specifically, can a noxious stimulus such as an electric shock serve as a UCS?
2. Will similar stimuli elicit the same response? If we have effectively conditioned a salivary response to a tuning fork of 1000 cycles per second (cps) will a dog also generalize this response to the sound of a tuning fork of 1200 cps? Will he salivate as much to a tuning fork of 1400 cps?
3. What is the best time interval between the onset of the CS and the onset of the UCS?
4. How can we build simple CS-CR connections into more complex units?

A Noxious Stimulus as a UCS

In his research, Pavlov almost always made use of a positive UCS such as food. W. von Bechterev, a Russian contemporary of Pavlov, initiated the study of electric shock, a noxious stimulus, as a UCS. In Bechterev's basic experiment he would touch a dog on his left rear paw (CS). An electric shock would then be administered to the right front paw (UCS), at which point the dog would automatically respond by flexing that paw (UCR). After a number of pairings of CS and UCS, the CS would be presented alone and a flexion of the right front paw (CR) would occur. Clearly, Bechterev had established an S-R connection between the touch on the left rear paw (CS) and flexion of the right front paw (CR). Notice that the dog did not avoid the shock by flexing his paw. Experimenters have also studied the effect of a CR that enables a subject to escape a shock. In this situation, it turns out, conditioning proceeds much more rapidly.

In a classic study, W.J. Brogden, E.A. Lipman, and Elmer Culler put two groups of four guinea pigs each in a rotating wire drum (squirrel cage). For both these groups (individually trained and tested), a tone (CS) was sounded followed by an electric shock (UCS), which caused the animals to run in the rotating cage (UCR). For one group, however, regardless of what they did, the shock was not turned off. After a number of such conditioning trials, according to the authors, the animals behaved as follows: "When the tone began, they [the guinea pigs] 'sat tight,' held their breath, and tensely awaited the shock." Some of the animals never learned to run (CR) to the sound of the tone. They all seemed to have learned to fear it.

In contrast the second group of guinea pigs, subjected to the same procedure, could turn off the shock if they succeeded in turning the rotating cage by running (UCR). Figure 3-3 shows in percentages how many animals in both groups learned the CR (running) to the sound of the tone.

The results show that in the early portion of the experiment both groups ran (CR) to the same extent when the tone was sounded. Those in the group that could avoid the shock continued to learn so that in eight days they were running 100 per cent of the time in response to the CS. In the group that could not avoid the shock, however, running did not increase in frequency as the experiment progressed. These animals, though, did learn an emotional re-

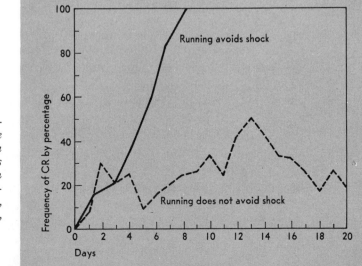

Figure 3-3. Comparison of learning where CR avoids shock with learning where CR does not avoid shock. (From W.J. Brogden, E.A. Lipman, and Elmer Culler, Amer. J. Psychol., 1938, 51, 110.)

action—fear—to the sound of the tone, as is evidenced by their crouching and breath-holding. This experiment has some of the properties of operant conditioning, which will be discussed below. It indicates that a negative stimulus, such as shock, may be used as a UCS to produce a conditioned response. If an animal's overt response serves to avoid the shock, then he learns the response more easily.

The Learning of Fear.   The most famous demonstration of classical conditioning of fear was reported by John B. Watson and Rosalie Rayner. A nine-month-old infant named Albert served as the subject. Initially, Albert was shown a tame white rat, which on first seeing only aroused the child's curiosity. After Albert had had a chance to examine the rat, the animal was removed from his sight. Then the rat was presented again, and at the same time the experimenter sounded an alarming noise (the pounding of a steel bar with a hammer) behind Albert. This noise frightened the boy and caused him to cry. After pairing the presentation of the rat with the harsh noise for about five trials, the experimenters again presented the rat alone. This time the sight of the rat was sufficient to make Albert cry.

If we substitute the Pavlovian terminology of CS for the rat, UCS for the harsh noise, and UCR (and later CR) for the child's crying, we have a model of how an infant may learn fear through conditioning. We can again affirmatively answer the question "Can a negative stimulus such as a shock, or harsh noise, be used as a UCS to produce a conditioned response?" We may further say that if an animal or person is unable to avoid a noxious UCS then he will not learn a specific motor response to a high degree of proficiency. He will, however, learn to fear the originally neutral *CS*. If escape from the *UCS* is possible, then he will develop an appropriate motor response.

Generalization

Stimulus Generalization.   The troubles of poor little Albert did not come to end when the white rat was removed from his sight, for now, not only did the sight of the white rat frighten him, but other objects such as a ball of cotton, or a rabbit, or a white mask, also frightened him. Albert was not frightened by any object that did not resemble the white rat (say, a block of wood), but he was by objects that were similar to it in some way (being white and fuzzy). For the sake of continuity, we shall leave Albert in this state of fear; it will be alleviated a few pages ahead.

Such a response, based on stimulus similarity, is called *stimulus generalization.* As in the case of Albert, we find that after a response is trained to a stimulus, similar stimuli can also elicit the response. In a very strict sense, generalization is always with us since we never experience the same stimulus in exactly the same way more than just once. Each time we walk down the street and enter the correct door to our residence our retina is doubtless stimulated in a different manner. This may be due to changes in light levels because of weather, time of day, or whether or not we are wearing sunglasses. It may be due to the exact angle at which we enter the street and approach our residence. In any case we are responding to a "new" stimulus which is similar to the stimulus situation in which we learned our response—our defining condition for stimulus generalization.

Generalization is an extremely important phenomenon; psychologists use it quite extensively to help explain other and more complex behavior. It has been called on to help explain aspects of the behavior of schizophrenics, behavior of various cultures, the Rorschach test, and psychotherapy, among other things. For this reason a great deal of research has been undertaken in order to describe generalization precisely. Many investigators have centered their attention on specifying the changes in response that result from varying the similarity of a test stimulus to a CS. The initial step in these studies has been to determine stimulus similarity. The most straightforward manner of doing so is to measure the closeness of stimuli on some physical scale. Thus, the hue orange is closer to red than green is; the note A is closer to B than E is; among sandpapers, grade 00 is more like grade 01 than grade 09 is; the back is closer to the shoulder than the ankle is. Generalized responses based on such measurable physical similarity are called *primary stimulus generalizations*. Our little friend Albert exhibited primary stimulus generalization in responding to test stimuli on the basis of their physical similarity to the original trained CS.

Most research on generalization uses a much more exacting measure. Pavlov, using a vibration applied to the *shoulder* of a dog as a CS and food as a UCS, found the spatial pattern of generalization presented in Table 3.

TABLE 3

Spatial Pattern of Stimulus Generalization in Dogs

Place Stimulated	Number of Drops of Saliva in 30 Seconds
Front paw	6
Shoulder (CS)	8
Side near shoulder	7
Side near thigh	3
Thigh	0
Hind paw	0

From I.P. Pavlov, *Conditioned reflexes* (trans. by G.V. Anrep). London: Oxford Univ. Press, 1927.

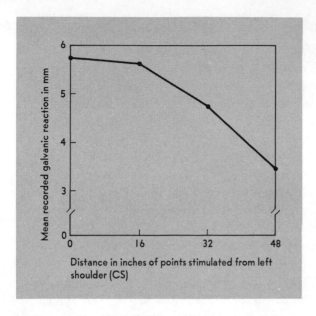

Figure 3-4.   A gradient of stimulus generalization obtained by Bass and Hull. (From M. Bass and C.L. Hull, J. comp. Psychol., 1934.)

The salivary response was the UCR and the CR. As the physical location of a test stimulus becomes more distant from the location of the original CS, the strength of the CR decreases.

Marjorie Bass and Clark Hull conducted this same experiment with male college students. Instead of salivation they used the galvanic skin response (GSR) as the CR. The GSR mentioned in Chapter 2 reflects a general state of emotionality, tension, or excitement. When we are emotional our autonomic nervous system becomes active. One of the results of such activity is increased sweating. Thus, as we become more emotional we sweat; as we sweat the electrical resistance of our skin decreases. This decrease in skin resistance can be observed with proper instruments, so it has frequently been measured as a CR. In the Bass and Hull study (as in Pavlov's) a vibration to the left shoulder was the CS. Immediately following the onset of this stimulus they administered an electric shock to the subject's right wrist and observed the conditioned GSR in the subject's left hand. After conditioning they tested for generalization by applying vibratory stimuli to the small of the student's back, left thigh, and left calf, each point exactly 16 inches from the one nearest it. The amount of response elicited by each of these locations is shown in Figure 3-4. This curve is called the *gradient of stimulus generalization*.

Stimulus Generalization and the Displacement of Emotion.   It would be a pity to leave this description of stimulus generalization without indicating one of the ways it has been used in explaining more complex behavior. Let us examine Neal Miller's analysis of *displacement*. Displacement is the name we give to the behavior of a boy who goes home and shouts at his little sister after quietly taking a severe scolding by his teacher at school. It consists of transferring a response from an original target to one that is more available or safer. If the sister then turns and kicks the dog, we have another example of displacement. Displacement is a concept that has seen wide use in the study of personality; it was first described by Sigmund Freud. As a subject for this discussion let us take a young lady's courtship problems. As will quickly become obvious, this analysis attempts to explain only one of the many influences on her courtship behavior. In addition, we shall center on only part of Miller's theoretical discussion.

As any parent can tell you, the first object of a little girl's affection is her father. Her later reactions to men are in some degree influenced by the similarity of these men to her father. This reaction on the basis of similarity is an instance of generalization. We might depict it in terms of a gradient as in Figure 3-5. The gradient is depicted as a straight line for purposes of clarity in the more complex figures that follow. The men in Figure 3-5 vary in terms of their similarity to the father. As a dimension of similarity we have arbitrarily chosen to consider only eye color in order to eliminate needless detail. We could, of course, use any other important physical dimension, such as hair color or height, or any more complex dimension such as friendliness or outgoingness. To be truly realistic we would have to use some weighted average of all relevant dimensions.

If our young lady were presented with this array of men proposing marriage, which would she pick? To begin with, thoughts relating to the father's candidacy would be accompanied by massive anxiety because of our civilization's powerful incest taboos. Would her choice then be Man 1? Well, because of Man 1's great similarity to the father, he shares, through generalization, more of the anxiety-avoidance relating to the incest taboo than the other

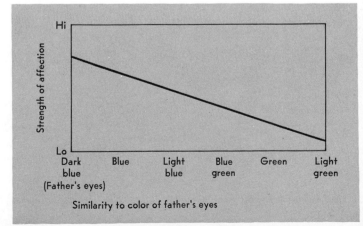

Figure 3-5. Stimulus generalization of a girl's affection response to her father.

suitors. The generalization gradient of this anxiety-avoidance response is shown along with the gradient for generalization of the approach response in Figure 3-6. Let us stop to point out a few features of this figure. To begin with, notice that the father elicits more avoidance than approach. This is in accordance with the dominance of the incest taboo. Notice also that the avoidance curve descends more rapidly (greater slope) than the approach curve. This is in accordance with results of research comparing the slopes of approach and avoidance generalization curves. In order to determine what she is likely to do, we must only subtract one gradient from the other at any point in question. She will choose the man whose resultant *approach* remainder is highest. In this case it is Man 2.

Stimulus Generalization, Displacement, and Prejudice.   This analysis relates to any situation in which displacement of responses might occur. The boy in the first example did not respond in kind to his teacher because of the dominance of his fear toward her. His little sister evoked little fear and enough hostility generalized from the teacher to be the subject of a displaced reaction. In this case the approach gradient refers to the hostility response. Research has suggested that racial prejudice is especially high in individuals who have had a good deal of harsh punishment in childhood. This punishment would serve to raise the level of fear-avoidance toward parents and consequently raise the entire generalization gradient for fear-avoidance which stems from the parents, as is shown in Figure 3-7. If hostility is aroused it will have to be massive in order to overcome the fear felt toward the parents. More likely it will be displaced out on the gradient to individuals in out-groups such as other races and religions.

Secondary Generalization.   Until now we have only spoken of primary generalization on the basis of physical similarity. Stimuli may be similar on other bases as well. For example, the words "baby" and "infant" have little physical similarity but are nevertheless alike in a clearly recognizable way.

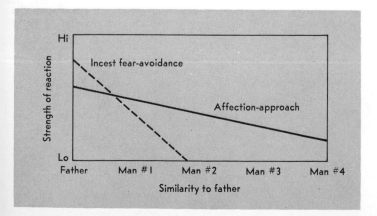

Figure 3-6. Interaction of generalization gradients of a girl's incest fear and affection response to her father.

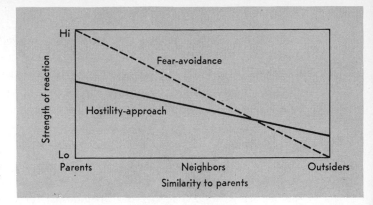

Figure 3-7. Displacement: interaction of generalization gradients of fear and hostility.

This sort of similarity is based on learning. Responses based on learned similarity are termed *secondary generalization.*

Gregory Razran attempted to study secondary generalization of salivation in human beings. He sat college students before a table laden with salty tidbits and asked them to munch away while words were being flashed on a screen. He assumed that the words would become CS's while the tidbits were UCS's—that is, in response to these UCS's and in the presence of the words, the students would salivate. Afterwards he tested to see whether conditioning had occurred by inserting wads of dental cotton into the students' mouths while the CS words and other, neutral words were exposed. The wads that were in the subjects' mouths while the CS's were flashed, turned out to weigh more than the others, thus indicating salivary conditioning. Razran also noted that when he tested with synonyms of the CS's he could detect a degree of salivation indicative of secondary generalization.

Discrimination

Although generalization is of great help to people, unless it is controlled it can lead into difficulties. Take the case of the new lieutenant in the army who says, "Good morning, Captain," to the major. Although the uniform of a captain and major are similar, there are important differences that the new lieutenant must learn to distinguish. The bases of such *discrimination* have been carefully studied. The first systematic investigations took place in Pavlov's laboratory. It happened this way.

Pavlov found that he could use almost any stimulus as a CS. He even trained a dog to salivate to a metronome ticking at 100 beats per minute. As we might expect from our knowledge of generalization, the dog also salivated to 80 beats per minute. Then Pavlov continued to deliver meat powder with the 100-beat CS, but not with the 80-beat stimulus. After giving a few responses to the 80-beat stimulus, the dog stopped; but he did continue to respond to the 100-beat one. The dog had *discriminated* the 100 beats from the 80 beats. In further training the 100-beat ticking was always followed by meat powder, but in the trial without meat powder Pavlov shifted to an 85-beat stimulus. After a few trials the dog again salivated only to the 100-beat sound. The dog's discrimination was then further tested by moving up to 90 beats and finally to 96 beats. Even with so small a difference as four beats per minute, the dog was still able to distinguish between the two rates.

Experimental Neurosis.   If the discrimination demanded became too fine, the dog semed to have a "nervous breakdown," or what Pavlov called *experimental neurosis*. Pavlov describes how he trained dogs to discriminate a circle from an ellipse. The circle was always positive (followed by the UCS, meat powder). The ratio between the horizontal and vertical diameters of the ellipse began at 2:1. As the discrimination experiment progressed, the ellipse was brought closer and closer to the circle. When the ellipse ratio reached 9:8, dogs became extremely disturbed and disorganized. They also lost the benefit of all their previous training, and responded at random to either circle or ellipse.

This result has been repeated in a number of laboratories. One essential feature of these procedures seems to be that the animal falls into a state of extreme conflict over whether or not to respond. Experiments conducted by Jules Masserman underline the role of conflict in experimental neuroses. He trained cats to open a box to obtain food. After training, the hungry cats encountered a sharp air blast when opening the box. Terrified of the air blast, but wanting the food, the cats exhibited extremely "neurotic" behavior. Masserman used the situation to test various treatments for the disturbance. He took the position that this experimentally produced disturbed behavior is similar to the neurotic behavior of human beings. We could also emphasize the importance of the *differences* between the restricted animal experiments and the possibility of rich variety of neuroses brought about by the symbolic and verbal abilities of people. Through secondary generalization the human being can find conflict in situations far removed from the area of original training. Despite this difference, there have been some useful attempts at understanding human neurotic behavior in terms of the basic laws of learning. Outstanding in this regard is a book by John Dollard and Neal Miller, *Personality and Psychotherapy*.

The Fate of the Conditioned Response

Extinction of the Conditioned Response.   When the dog was able to discriminate, he withheld responses save for the 100-beat stimulus. Pavlov effected this suppression of response by omitting the UCS when stimuli other than the 100-beat stimulus were presented. After a number of presentations of the CS alone, the CR to it will fail to occur. This process of eliminating a CR is called *extinction*.

Another way to reduce the number of CR's to a CS is to introduce a loud noise simultaneously with, or just following the presentation of the CS. That this type of inhibition called *external inhibition,* occurs so easily is the main reason for doing conditioning studies in relatively soundproofed areas. What may happen is that the novel stimulus momentarily changes the nature of the total stimulus condition just enough to produce a temporary reduction in the strength of the CR.

If a novel stimulus is introduced while an experimenter is attempting to extinguish a CR, a temporary *increase* in the strength of the faltering CR occurs. Pavlov believed this demonstrated that CR's were not irreparably lost during extinction, rather that they were inhibited by other factors. He believed that the introduction of a novel stimulus served to remove this inhibition. For this reason he gave the name *disinhibition,* or inhibition of inhibition to this sudden rise in the strength of a CR undergoing extinction. Through the phenomena of *spontaneous recovery* Pavlov found further evidence for the claim that the CR was not totally unlearned during extinction. If a period of rest was given to an animal after supposedly complete extinction, the CR would again appear without further training. Furthermore, the strength of the CR after the rest would be almost as great as its strength before extinction. If the animal is continually put through the cycle of extinction and spontaneous recovery, the spontaneous recovery that occurs becomes less and less at each cycle. Eventually the response will not recover at all.

We can now trace the CR through four stages: conditioning, extinction, rest, and spontaneous recovery. Figure 3-8 presents a schematic outline of this

Figure 3-8. *Stages in the conditioning and extinction of a conditioned response.*

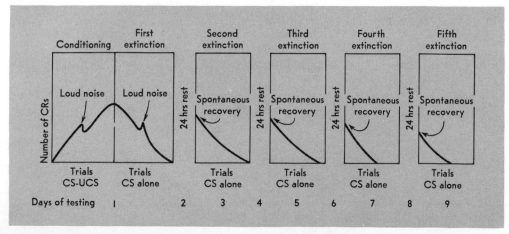

process. Note that we have included a number of rest and extinction periods after the initial conditioning and extinction period. Note, in addition, that the initial amount of spontaneous recovery decreases after each extinction period.

Another way of eliminating a conditioned response is to train an incompatible response to the same stimulus. This is the way Albert was cured of his fear of the white rat. First the caged rat was brought into the same room as Albert but moved away until Albert could tolerate its presence without whimpering. While Albert kept track of the rat out of the corner of his eye, he was plied with his favorite dessert. The next day the rat was moved a little bit closer while Albert happily ate. Notice that Albert was manifesting a "happiness" response in the presence of the rat and this response was incompatible with crying. After a number of such sessions the rat and Albert were happily reunited. This technique is ideal for retraining children. One caution, however: The situation must be handled with finesse. Rather than teach Albert to be happy with the rat the experimenters might have caused him to fear the dessert.

Variations on the Theme:
Temporal Relations between CS and UCS

Up to this point we have considered only the case where the UCS occurs either at the same time as, or just following, the onset of the CS. This type is called *simultaneous conditioning*. But beyond this, nearly all possible temporal relations have been used in conditioning research. Each has a name, as the diagrams in Figure 3-9 show. The top line in each part indicates the CS. A rise in this line denotes the

Figure 3-9.   Relationship between CS and UCS in four types of conditioning.

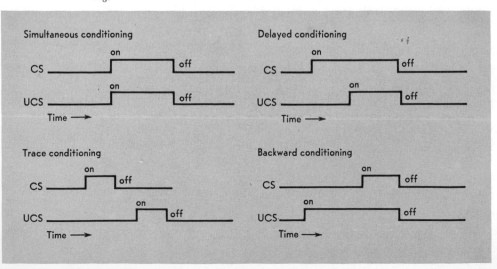

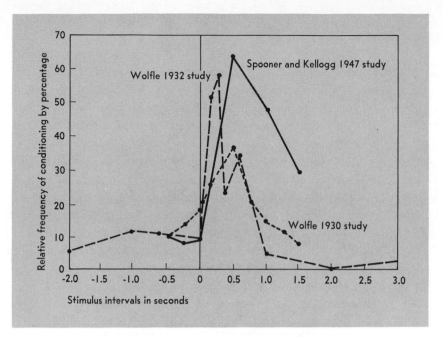

Figure 3-10. Comparison of the effectiveness of different CS-UCS intervals. (From A. Spooner and W.N. Kellogg, Amer. J. Psychol., 1947, 60, 327.)

onset of the CS. The lower line of the pair indicates the UCS and here too a rise indicates the onset of the UCS. A drop in a line indicates the termination of each stimulus.

Which of these experimental set-ups leads to the easiest learning of a CR? As you might expect, the simultaneous condition is the best, but, what might be surprising, exact simultaneity of CS and UCS is not best. Virtually all investigators have reported that a delay of about half a second between the onset of the CS and the onset of the UCS produces the fastest learning. On either side of this interval conditioning proceeds more slowly. In an early experiment on these time relations, Helen M. Wolfle found that having the CS precede the UCS by .5 second was best. The most complete study on this topic was that of A. Spooner and W.M. Kellogg, who worked with the following five temporal intervals between CS and UCS: —.5 sec., —.25 sec., +.5 sec., +1.0 sec., and +1.5 sec. (the negative numbers indicate *backward conditioning* when the UCS preceded the CS). In Figure 3-10 we see a composite of the results of Wolfle and of Spooner and Kellogg. Again we see that the optimal interval between the CS and UCS is about +.5 sec. This persistent and specific time relation, intriguing as it is, has thus far eluded complete explanation.

Higher-order Conditioning

A number of psychologists believe that classical conditioning is the basic form of learning. These individuals argue that all other learning stems from it, more complex behavior simply consisting of series of conditioned responses and *higher-order conditioned responses*. In the latter type of conditioning a CS from one situation is used as the UCS in another. Glen Finch and Elmer Culler conducted classic experiments on this topic. First they trained a dog to withdraw his paw in order to avoid a shock when a tone was presented. After some training along these lines, the tone was paired with a light; the light soon became an effective CS, eliciting withdrawal of the paw. A jet of water on the dog's nose was then paired with the light and it too became an effective CS as did a bell and finally a fan. Such successful higher-order conditioning has not been obtained with salivation as the CR, however. Perhaps the electric shock produces fear that becomes a stimulus capable of eliciting withdrawal of the paw. If so, it is then possible that the fear response was being conditioned to each of the new CS's and that this was partially responsible for the success of this instance of higher-order conditioning.

The Conditioning of Meaning, an Instance of Higher-order Conditioning. A recent adaptation of higher-order conditioning principles begins on the assumption that the connotative (for example, emotional) meanings of some words may be learned through classical conditioning. Thus, it is quite likely that a child learns the meaning of the word *bad* because he is generally punished after some act of his has been labelled "bad." In this case the word *bad* is the CS, punishment is the UCS, and some emotional response such as "feeling unpleasant" is the CR. After a number of pairings of *bad* with punishment, *bad* itself should begin to arouse conditioned unpleasant feelings in the absence of physical punishment. Now if the child is told that "dirt is bad," on the basis of higher-order conditioning procedures, the word *dirt* takes on some of *bad*'s unpleasant feelings.

This is a plausible hypothesis; some recent work has shown that we may indeed acquire meanings in much this way. One experiment by Arthur and Carolyn Staats has shown that if you pair a nonsense syllable such as WEM with a group of unpleasant words such as bad, mean, and sour, the syllable takes on unattractive overtones; if you pair it with words such as love, peace, and sweet, it comes to be rated as pleasant. Although work of this type is still in its infancy, it shows promise of providing a partial answer to the problem of how words and objects acquire their emotional significance.

The scene is an interview room in a mental hospital. A seriously disturbed patient is discussing his mental status with a psychologist. The psychologist says almost nothing in response to the patient's remarks except for an occasional approving "yes" or understanding "uh-huh," responses meant to be reinforcements. And he does so only when the patient makes a statement of opinion, such as "I feel that . . . ," or "It is my conviction that. . . ." What is the result of this procedure? Experimenters Kurt Salzinger and Stephanie Pisoni discovered that the reinforcement provided by such statements of social approval are effective in greatly increasing the number of opinion statements made by patients. (Although the point is not directly relevant to our discussion of conditioning, it is of incidental interest that the patients who condition more easily, recover from their illness more quickly. Perhaps this is because they are more sensitive to the reinforcement provided by such social approval.)

Similar experiments have been conducted with normal persons. In one form, the experimenter instructs a subject to call out any word that comes to mind. Whenever the subject calls out a word that belongs to an arbitrarily selected category such as plural nouns or two-syllable words, the experimenter responds with an encouragement such as "uh-huh." A record of the occurrence of responses in the preselected category as a function of time (say, number of plural nouns in successive one-minute periods) will typically show that the *rate of emission* of these responses increases markedly as the experiment continues. This conditioning can occur apparently even if the subject does not become aware of the rationale of the procedure. If he is aware, conditioning proceeds more rapidly. Some recent data suggest that a careful postexperimental interview discloses that all subjects who condition have some level of awareness of the experimental contingencies.

The essential elements here are a response that is already available to the subject (plural nouns) and a stimulus (uh-huh) that is effective in increasing the strength of that response. The response is called an *operant response* (it operates to bring about the reinforcement), the strengthening stimulus is called a *reinforcer,* and the general procedure is called *operant conditioning.* As we saw earlier, this is the type of conditioning that enabled the student to bring the mental patient to the basement experiment room.

Perhaps the most well-known apparatus used for operant conditioning is a small, sometimes airconditioned, sometimes soundproofed, box that contains a little lever, a food cup, and perhaps a light. This apparatus is called a

"Boy, have I got this guy conditioned! Every time I press the bar down he drops in a piece of food."

Figure 3-11. A typical Skinner Box? (Adapted, by permission, from Jester, *Columbia University.)*

Skinner Box, after B.F. Skinner, the man who invented it and first described the process of operant conditioning (see Figure 3-11). Typically the lever in the Skinner Box is connected to a recording pen. This pen rests and writes on a constantly moving strip of paper; when no response is occurring the pen simply draws a horizontal line. To record the occurrence of each lever response, the pen makes a small upward movement. When after many upward movements it reaches the top of the paper it usually is automatically reset to the bottom of the page and can begin again. An example of the data generated by this apparatus is presented in Figure 3-12, which is a *cumulative response graph.* Note that the ordinate (vertical axis) in Figure 3-12 denotes

Figure 3-12. A typical cumulative response graph showing a record of the first four responses. A and B denote slope—hence, rate—of responses.

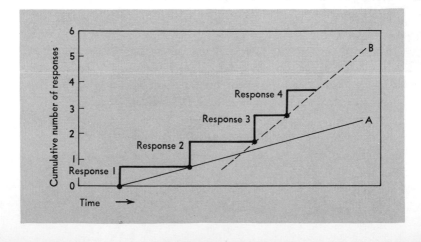

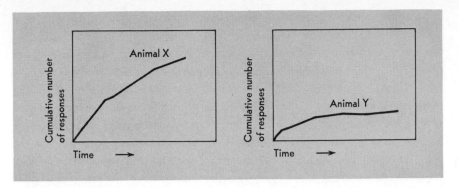

Figure 3-13. *A comparison of the response rates of two rats pushing a lever for food.*

the total cumulative number of responses whereas the abscissa (horizontal axis) presents a continuous record of time. There are four responses on this graph, each of which is indicated by an upward deflection. The graph shows many things. For one, obviously the time between responses 3 and 4 is less than the time between responses 1 and 2. For another, the steepness of the slope between any two points tells the rate of response. Here, the solid line labeled A denotes the slope between responses 1 and 2, the dotted line labeled B denotes the slope between responses 3 and 4. Since the slope of line B is steeper than the slope of line A, the rate of response between 3 and 4 is faster than the rate between 1 and 2.

It is possible to compare differences in response rate for different animals with such graphs—the steeper the slope the faster the response rate. In Figure 3-13 we see graphs for two rats pushing a lever for food. Animal X's response rate is considerably faster than animal Y's rate as is shown by the steeper slope of X's curve. Such a difference might result if X is hungrier than Y.

Schedules of Reinforcement

"The fisherman does not hook a fish with every cast of the line; the crop the farmer sows does not always yield a harvest." And the rat does not get a pellet every time he presses the lever—reinforcement does not always occur 100 per cent of the time. The operant conditioner will often only reinforce once for every other response, or once for every ten responses, or even once for every 50 responses. We use the term *partial reinforcement* to indicate such situations. When the partial reinforcement is regular (say, once every ten responses), we call it *ratio reinforcement.* Interesting results occur when the partial reinforcement is keyed to time. *Interval reinforcement,* as this is called, does not depend on the number of responses made; an experimenter simply reinforces one response in a time period (for example, one response every minute). No matter how many responses are made only the first one will be reinforced in any given one-minute period. These different *schedules of reinforcement* (100 per cent, ratio, interval) each yield different and characteristic patterns of behavior. What human behavior depends on reinforcements of one kind or the other? Consider the victim of the partial reinforcement schedule doled out by a one-armed bandit at Las Vegas. Consider the workers who are paid a given amount of money for a given number of tons of coal dug or seams sewed.

Effects of Partial Reinforcement

In first training a subject to give a response, it is most efficient to supply a reinforcement with every response. Under partial reinforcement, training is prolonged, but a response trained under partial reinforcement will continue long after reinforcement stops. A response trained under 100 per cent reinforcement extinguishes quickly when reinforcement stops. The dramatic resistance to extinction exhibited by animals trained under partial reinforcement is shown in Figure 3-14. This figure shows the cumulative number of responses made by two groups of animals, one trained on a 100 per cent schedule, one on an interval schedule. The animals in both groups received 200 reinforcements before extinction began. As is shown by the number of responses made before complete ex-

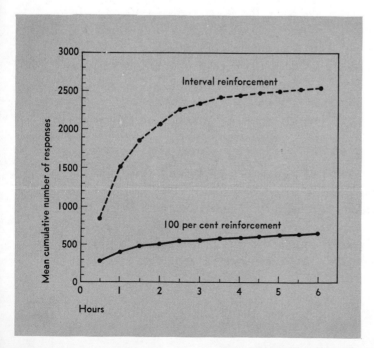

Figure 3-14. The effects of 100 per cent reinforcement and interval reinforcement on the number of trials to extinction. (From W.O. Jenkins, H. McFann, and F.L. Clayton, J. comp. physiol. Psychol., 1950, 43, 155–167, p. 158.)

Figure 3-15. The number of unrewarded responses is shown as a function of the percentage of reinforcement subjects received in training. (From D.J. Lewis and C.P. Duncan, J. exp. Psychol., 1958, 55, 121–128, p. 123.)

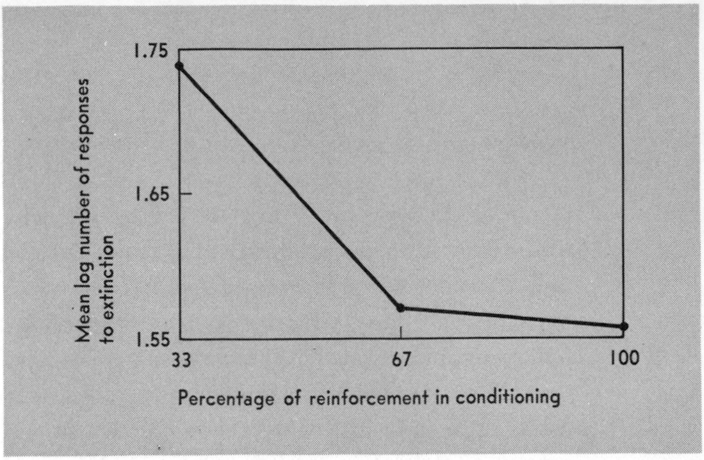

tinction occurs, the partially reinforced group is considerably more persistent than the other group.

Quite similar results have been obtained in research with human beings. Donald J. Lewis and Carl P. Duncan rescued a condemned slot machine (one-armed bandit) from the axe of a crusading Cook County Sheriff and ingeniously adapted it to study the effects of partial reinforcement. The device was built to take quarters. As a consequence subjects were provided with a large supply of quarter-sized discs and told that they could play the slot machine as long as they pleased. The experimenters varied the percentage of reinforcement during training between 33 and 100. Each disc the subjects won could later be cashed in for a nickel. After training, no further reinforcements were given; the number of trials until the subject quit was then automatically recorded. Figure 3-15 shows the number of unrewarded responses subjects made as a function of the percentage of reinforcement they received in training. Again we see the potent effects of partial reinforcement as compared with 100 per cent reinforcement.

How should we interpret this finding? Whether a person gives a previously learned response depends on the similarity of the test situation to the training situation (recall the principles of stimulus generalization). Since in training the partial reinforcement group gives many responses that are not followed by reinforcement, the extinction period is not a great change for them. But it is a dramatic change for the 100 per cent reinforcement group. Therefore, the partial reinforcement group continues to respond for a longer period of time when reinforcement is discontinued.

These findings have clear implications for child training. When we first try to teach a child to perform an act we should reinforce him liberally. As the child gains skill in the act, reinforcement should taper off. By tapering off we assure the response a long life even when we are not nearby to apply frequent reinforcements.

Superstitious Behavior in Pigeons
and the Shaping of Behavior

You can make pigeons chronically hungry by feeding them a reduced diet until they stay at 80 per cent of normal body weight. In this condition food as a reinforcement has a dramatic effect on whatever behavior it follows. In one of his experiments, Skinner placed hungry pigeons, one at a time, in a Skinner Box and delivered reinforcements at random intervals.

A pigeon tended to seize upon and repeat frequently whatever behavior it was engaged in just before the reinforcement. (Note the similarity of these pigeons to the behavior of the Olds and Milner "historic" rat that repeated behavior which had, by chance, been reinforced by the electrical brain stimulation.) As likely as not, then, this behavior would occur just about at the time of the next random delivery of food and so would be reinforced again. Soon this behavior dominated the pigeon's activity. Skinner likens the pigeon's "beliefs" to superstitious notions that people learn as a result of the chance joint occurrence of an act and a reinforcement. The primitive farmer does a dance and it rains. He dances again and again in the hope that this will bring the rain again. Once in a while the dance is followed by reinforcement. Under such conditions of partial reinforcement it is difficult to extinguish the dance response and belief. Henceforth he believes that doing this dance brings on the rain. Plainly, a reinforcement can be an influential event.

Since reinforcement is so effective in controlling behavior, psychologists have used it to teach animals all sorts of tricks. One such demonstration is shown in the following picture. The duck has been trained through the use of positive reinforcement and the principles of response *shaping*. Response shaping is the process of rewarding responses that approximate the desired response. For example, if an experimenter wanted a dog to go to a wall, he would make the animal hungry and then give him some food for every response that tended to bring him closer to the wall. Initially the experimenter would reinforce any tendency in the appropriate direction, later only definite responses in that direction. In this way the animal would tend to go to the wall in a series of steps that gradually approached the desired response. In the first chapter, another example of response shaping was presented, one involving a mental patient. The principles in both cases are identical.

In almost all fields, such as academic teaching or psychological counseling, where the goal is to teach responses of one kind or another the concept of *shaping* is used. Before a response may be shaped, however, a child or patient must have an appropriate readiness for the task. *Readiness* is a matter of having available the responses required for a task. Readiness may be either

Figure 3-16. The piano-playing duck turns on the lamp when given the signal, and then on a fixed ratio schedule plays a sequence up and down the keyboard on the piano. (From Animal Behavior Enterprises.)

physical or psychological. For example, in order to be able to learn to read, a child must be physically ready for the conditions of the task—that is, he must have eye coordination, be visually capable of discriminating among letters, and so on. Shaping *then* can provide a technique for gradually getting responses to occur in the desired situation and with the appropriate level of reliability.

An Example
of Research in Operant Conditioning

As we have seen, an organism trained to give a certain response to a stimulus will give this response to similar stimuli. This process of stimulus generalization has been explored primarily through classical conditioning procedures. Using operant conditioning techniques Norman Guttman and Harry Kalish studied it in pigeons. One question they specifically investigated was this: If you condition a pigeon to respond to a light of a given color (pigeons have excellent color vision), how far will its generalization extend from that color? First, they trained a hungry pigeon to peck at a translucent light key (see Figure 3-17 which presents a schematic diagram of the apparatus used in this experiment), and reinforced the bird with food for doing so. Then by tilting the diffraction grating, they varied the color of the key. They expected that pigeons would

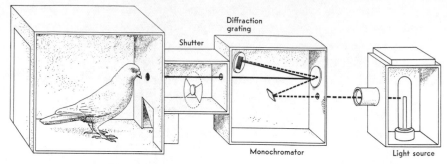

Figure 3-17.   *Experimental apparatus used to test for generalization in the pigeon. The color of light seen by the pigeon on the translucent light key in front of its beak is changed by tilting the diffraction grating with respect to the beam of light. The shutter enables the experimenter to black out the light while changing colors. (From N. Guttman, and H.I. Kalish,* Sci. Amer., *1958, 198, 78–79. Reprinted with permission. Copyright © 1958 by Scientific American, Inc. All rights reserved.)*

Figure 3-18.   *Generalization gradients obtained in pigeons for four differently colored initial stimuli (shown by arrows). (From Guttman and Kalish.)*

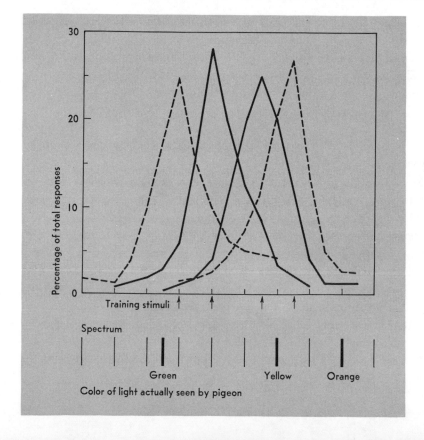

generalize within the same band as the original training color; thus, a bird trained to respond to a wavelength corresponding to a deep green would also respond to a wavelength corresponding to a lighter green. On this assumption they hypothesized that generalization would not "jump the color"; that is, if the conditioning stimulus were green, the animal would not generalize to a pure yellow light. Notice that the *names* given to these particular bands of wavelength originated with human beings.

The results did not support this particular hypothesis. Rather than show any irregularity correlated with the names of the colors, the gradients of generalization in pigeons proceed quite regularly along with the dimension of wavelength. In Figure 3-18 we see four different gradients of generalization, each stemming from original training at a specific wavelength. In all four cases the generalization gradients are regular and symmetrical around the original training light. Even when the gradient crosses color boundaries (as human beings perceive them) it remains smooth. As Guttman and Kalish noted:

> The curve of response was quite orderly: fast pecking at wavelengths close to the training stimulus, diminishing rates of pecking at more distant wavelengths. It was as if the pigeons were equipped with a frequency analyser, accurately identifying each wavelength. In other words they possess something like absolute pitch in the visual spectrum.

We have considered the simplest type of learning under two broad headings: Classical Conditioning and Operant Conditioning. Let us summarize what we have discussed so far.

Classical Conditioning

Salivation in dogs and the knee jerk in human beings are responses that occur automatically, without training, if an adequate sitmulus is presented. By pairing a neutral stimulus (CS) with the adequate stimulus (UCS), we can eventually make the response (CR) occur to the previously neutral stimulus alone. This process is called *classical conditioning*. Further, the response will also occur to a stimulus similar to the CS; we call this *stimulus generalization*. We have shown how stimulus generalization may be useful in the explanation of more complex human behavior. If we continue to present the CS without the benefit of the UCS, however, we will *extinguish* the CR. That is, it will no longer occur upon presentation of the CS. After a rest period, though, the CR will *spontaneously recover* from the effects of extinction. We reported the following facts:

1. Conditioning is fastest if the CS precedes the UCS by half a second.

2. Though the process is difficult, it is possible to use a CS as a UCS for a new neutral stimulus in order to produce *higher-order conditioning*.

By making use of higher-order conditioning, it is possible to explain more complex learning (for example, learning of the emotional meanings of words) on the basis of simple conditioning principles.

Operant Conditioning

In operant conditioning a response typically occurs without any prompting by a specific stimulus imposed by the experimenter. If it is followed by an appropriate reinforcing event, the strength and likelihood of this response will increase. The nature of responses conditioned by this procedure is extremely broad: vocal responses in human beings, bar-press responses in animals, key-pecking responses in pigeons, and so forth. Just as in classical conditioning, a response in operant conditioning can be extinguished by lack of reinforcement. If in the original training, however, every response was not reinforced (called *partial reinforcement*) extinction is considerably delayed.

CLASSICAL AND OPERANT CONDITIONING: A COMPARISON

You may have begun to wonder why we included separate discussions of classical and operant conditioning. They seem quite similar. Both are forms of conditioning. If you withhold the reinforcement or UCS, extinction occurs. Spontaneous recovery is a feature of both types of learning. In both we find external inhibition, disinhibition, stimulus generalization, discrimination, and higher-order conditioning. Indeed, the similarities are great.

Then what are the differences? First, the operational distinctions: In classical conditioning the occurrence of the conditioned response is *reflexively forced* by the UCS (salivation to the meat powder, galvanic skin response to the electric shock); in operant conditioning the response is more voluntary (pressing a bar, uttering a statement of opinion). A related point is that in classical conditioning the UCS occurs without regard to the subject's behavior, whereas in operant conditioning the reward is contingent on the occurrence of the response.

There are other differences. It is not a difficult matter to condition responses of the autonomic nervous system, such as the GSR or blood pressure changes, by classical conditioning methods. Yet this is apparently impossible with operant conditioning techniques. I once spent a month of afternoons dispensing nickels to an undergraduate every time he showed a spontaneous GSR. If the nickel reward had been contingent on some operant response such as bar-pressing, the rate of bar-pressing would have shown a marked increase in this period of time. But no noticeable change in the rate of GSR's occurred at the end of the month. Other researchers have also failed in attempting to condition a reaction of the autonomic nervous system by operant techniques. From such evidence some theorists have developed the idea that the central nervous system (more or less voluntary skeletal and muscular reactions) is controlled by operant conditioning, but that classical conditioning controls the autonomic nervous system (more or less emotional reactions). In apparent opposition to this point of view are the many instances in research reports of individuals who have learned voluntary control over such autonomic reactions as constriction and dilation of the pupil and the GSR. Even in these cases, however, the process merely involved the classical conditioning of the autonomic reaction to a stimulus the individual could voluntarily provide for himself—such as a word. This means that although producing the word was voluntary, the autonomic response to the word had been conditioned by classical methods. Applying the distinction between autonomic nervous system and central nervous system to classical and operant conditioning has a good deal of merit. There may be exceptions to this distinction but it provides a correct definition of the central emphases of both kinds of conditioning.

According to one line of theoretical thought, no reward is really necessary in classical conditioning. The UCS only functions to produce the CR in contiguity with the CS. All that is necessary is CS—CR contiguity. It has been maintained, however, that in operant conditioning the reward is *essential* for conditioning. Thus, classical conditioning is conditioning by the law of contiguity and operant conditioning is conditioning by the law of effect (reward). The argument with respect to classical conditioning is quite tenable. Yet, you will recall Brogden's 1962 demonstration (described in Chapter 2) that merely by presenting a tone in contiguity with an operant response (cage turning), effective conditioning of his kittens resulted. This evidence casts some doubt on the contiguity-reward distinction between the two types.

In summary, we can point to many similarities in operant and classical conditioning. In general terms the major difference seems to be that operant conditioning relates to learning that requires voluntary responses, whereas classical conditioning involves involuntary responses. More specifically, classical conditioning seems more appropriate for learning that involves emotional conditioning such as fear or anxiety (in which the autonomic nervous system is involved) while operant conditioning is more applicable to responses of the skeletal musculature or higher mental processes (in which the central nervous system is involved). All these distinctions should be understood as simply representing relative emphases. It is not easy to separate the two forms of learning completely. For example, try to design an operant conditioning study that has no components of classical conditioning in it.

Simple
Learning

Complex Habits

When an adult walks across a floor or reaches for an object, his behavior appears to proceed in a smooth uninterrupted stream. But slow motion movies of these behaviors would reveal that every act consists of many smaller ones. When you reach for something, for example, your arm is continually making slight adjustments to zero in on the desired object. This suggests that many sequential, or continuous, acts are actually composed of a string of smaller learned habits. Some intuitively apparent examples are provided by a child spelling a word or a student going through a geo-

54

4

metric proof. In this chapter we shall examine some factors that control the chaining together of the relatively simple type of learning discussed in Chapter 3.

Let us take a well-learned behavior sequence and analyze its characteristics. The recitation of the alphabet provides an example. First, note how rapidly and smoothly, and how free of halts or errors nearly everyone's performance is. A fourth-grade child can often recite it as an indistinct blur of sound of three seconds' duration. When serial behavior is accomplished in this manner, we say that *skill* has been acquired. Requiring the fourth-grader to recite the alphabet backward highlights the *directional character* of serial behavior. His time suddenly jumps to 45 seconds; and he must review parts of the alphabet in a forward direction to find his next response. A consideration of the alphabet also suggests that the later responses in a series are in large part determined by all the items that have come before. Benton J. Underwood and Rudolph W. Schulz have determined that if students are asked to give their first letter-association to the letter F, only 1.8 per cent answer G, but if asked to give their first letter-association to the combination $E\ F$, the proportion responding with G jumps by a factor of 10 to 18 per cent. Give the class $A\ B\ C\ D\ E\ F$ and G becomes the overwhelming choice for the next response. As the string of letters is increased the next item in the sequence becomes more inevitably determined. That placing $A\ B\ C\ D\ E$ before F increases the likelihood of G, suggests that G is partly determined by some small, remote S-R connections between each of these letters and G. Much the same sort of remote dependencies exist in other sequential, associative, and thought processes. A word in such a series can help determine a choice seven words ahead. (Interestingly enough, this is just about the average memory span; see Chapter 7.) Let us see what effect all these complex and remote connections have on serial learning.

Serial Learning in Animals

One night in 1934, at Yale University, after the students had deserted the psychology building, psychologists assembled in a long corridor to conduct an experiment with rats. They chose a long corridor because they had strung together seven straight and narrow runways, each six feet long, and the total length of 42 feet exceeded the size of their largest experimental room. They worked at night since they wished to keep the corridor empty while the rats were in the runways.

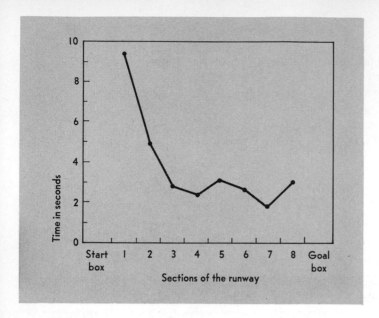

Figure 4-1. The goal gradient phenomenon in rats. This graph presents the amount of time in seconds it took a group of rats to cross each of the eight sections of a simple maze. (From C.L. Hull, J. comp. Psychol., 1934, 17, 393–422, p. 404.)

A *small* box was placed at each end of the 42-foot runway; one was the starting box and the other was the goal box. Hungry rats put in the starting box made their way down the runway to the goal box and food.

The hypothesis was that the effect of the food reward would be greatest at the goal box and would decrease with distance from it. Consequently, a rat's speed should increase as it moved down the runway. Each rat's progress across each section was timed and a curve (Figure 4-1) plotted of his speed.

As Figure 4-1 shows, as a rat approached the goal box, his speed of running increased, reached a maximum just before the goal box, and at the very end slowed down a bit. The slowing down at the end was caused by the small size of the goal box. The point is, if a rat rushed into the goal box at top speed, he would likely have crashed nose-first into the end wall. What is critical here is the demonstration of a general tendency for organisms to increase the vigor of their responses as they near a goal. This tendency is called a *goal gradient,* referring to the fact that the effect of a reward diminishes with time and distance from the goal. Experiments on this tendency provided our first hint that serial acts are not smooth, continuous sequences. The diminishing effectiveness of reward over time suggests that in training children a small reward at the moment a praiseworthy act occurs will go a lot farther in strengthening that act than a massive reward much later.

Investigators have also sought to chart errors as a function of the part of the act in which they occur. Results in the study of errors have been quite consistent in research with animals and men. In work with animals an apparatus similar to the one depicted in Figure 4-2 is common. This maze, used in an experiment by Clark Hull, had a series of four separate sections. The entrance to each section was divided into four doors. In order to complete the maze, a rat was required to go through a different door in each of the four sections. The rat received food only after completing the terminal section. The upper part of Figure 4-2 shows one possible pattern a rat had to learn in order to traverse the maze correctly. In this case, the rat had to go through door 1 (counting from the animal's left) in section 1, door 3 in section 2, door 2 in section 3, and door 4 in section 4. Did the 72 animals used in this study make a different number of errors at each of the four choice points?

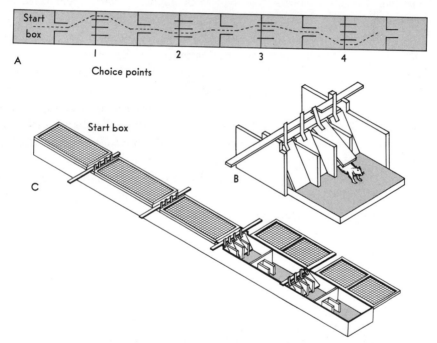

Figure 4-2.   Straight maze used to study serial learning in rats. Part A shows the floor plan of one possible route through the maze; B presents a closeup of one set of doors; while C shows the over-all nature of the maze. (From C.L. Hull and A.J. Sprow, J. exp. Psychol., *1947, 37, 118–135.)*

Figure 4-3 clearly shows that the number of errors differed at each of the choice points: Most errors were made at points 2 and 3, the least at points 1 and 4. Here then is more evidence of differences in the ease of learning various components of a serial task. Items at the beginning and at the end of a series are easier to learn than those in the middle positions. Similar results have been obtained with human beings, the principal tool in this study being the rote learning of a series of words.

Human Verbal Learning

In 1885, Hermann Ebbinghaus published a remarkable book of experiments on memory. What makes this book remarkable is that Ebbinghaus was both the sole experimenter and the sole subject in this entire series of experiments. For a period of about 20 years, Ebbinghaus learned, relearned, and memorized lists of nonsense syllables. These nonsense syllables, which you encountered in Chapter 1, were specifically invented for use in studying verbal learning and retention. For his purposes, they had to be simple to handle and construct. Because they were "meaningless," uncontrolled and previously learned responses were minimized. He constructed about 2,300 of them, writing out each consonant-vowel-consonant combination on a slip of paper. He would shuffle the slips and draw out between 12 and 18 slips before each experiment. As soon as he had learned a particular list of nonsense syllables, he put them back into the pool, reshuffled, and drew out another set. In each experiment, Ebbinghaus studied all the syllables at the same time, mastering each item in the list at his own rate. Consequently he spent more time on some syllables (the more difficult ones) than on others.

Today, however, experimenters generally present such materials to subjects by means of a memory drum (see Figure 4-4). With this device, items appear, one at a time, in the small opening. The amount of time a subject can spend on each item is constant, generally about two seconds. The subject's task is to anticipate the next item on the list. If he cannot anticipate the next syllable or

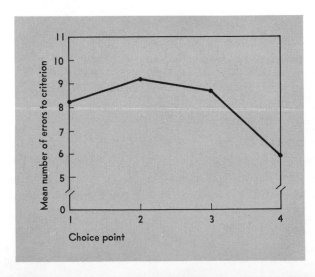

Figure 4-3. Number of errors made at 4 different choice points in a straight alley maze. (Adapted from G.A. Kimble, Hilgard and Marquis' conditioning and learning. New York: Appleton-Century-Crofts, 1961.)

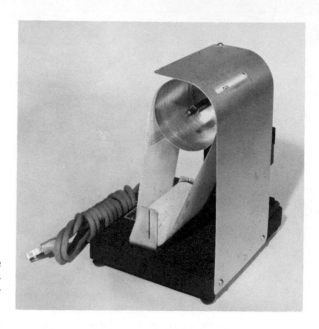

Figure 4-4. A simple memory drum. (Courtesy Ralph Gerbrands Co.)

makes an incorrect selection, the experimenter records the type of error. As we shall see later, the nature of these anticipatory errors tells us a great deal about the course of serial learning.

Serial Position Effect

We have mentioned a few phenomena that appear in serial learning by animals. In the Hull experiment, for instance, we found that the middle portion of a maze is most difficult to learn. This tendency also holds true for people learning serial lists of verbal materials. Probably one of the best demonstrations of this effect was presented by Carl I. Hovland. He had subjects learn a list which contained 12 nonsense syllables. He then counted the total number of errors each subject made at each of the 12 positions in the list. His results are shown in Figure 4-5, where you can see that the greatest number of errors occur with the syllable just past the middle of the series. This finding is called the *serial position effect*. If we compare this figure with Figure 4-1, which presents the results of a serial learning experiment done with rats, we see a similar serial position effect. In another experiment, using actual English sentences, the middle of the sentence proved to be the most difficult part for subjects to recall. It seems clear that the serial position effect shows up with a wide variety of both materials and subjects.

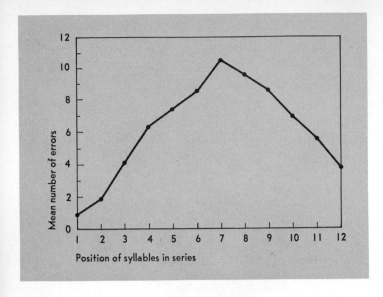

Figure 4-5. Mean number of errors made at different positions in a list of nonsense syllables. (From C.I. Hovland, J. exp. Psychol., 1938, 23, 172–190, p. 178.)

Spelling a word provides an interesting instance of the serial position effect. Arthur R. Jensen compared the effect for errors in spelling seven-, nine-, and eleven-letter words and the effect for errors in learning a series of nine colored geometric shapes. Figure 4-6 shows the serial position effect for both the nine-letter words and the nine-item list. The curves are quite similar. Jensen discarded the hypothesis that the spelling curve resulted from the ease of spelling prefixes and suffixes so that their location in a word might produce the effect artificially. He tested and found that these elements elicited about the same number of errors as the other parts of words. Further, only a small proportion of the words he used had prefixes or suffixes.

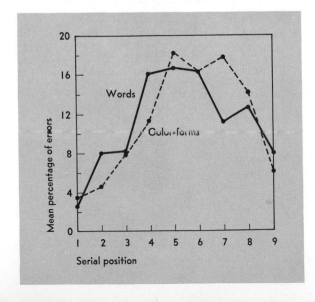

Figure 4-6. Comparison of the serial position effect for spelling errors and for learning a series of color forms. (From A.R. Jensen, J. educ. Psychol., 1962, 53, 105–109, p. 107.)

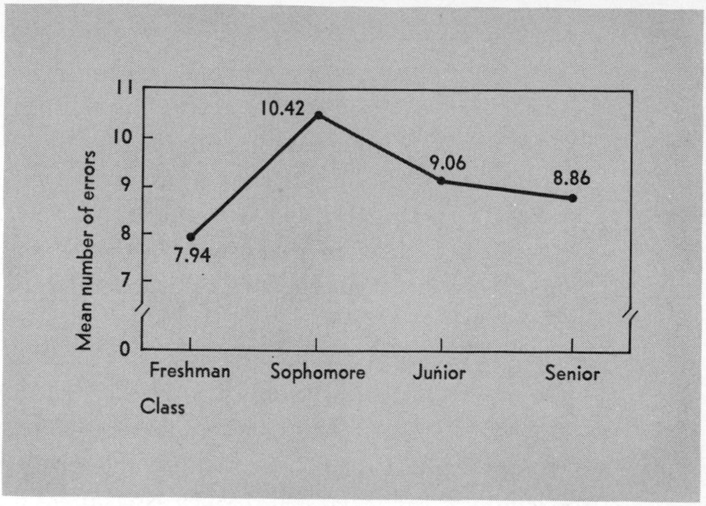

Figure 4-7. Mean number of errors made to each of the class labels. (From C.B. DeSoto and J.J. Bosley, The cognitive structure of a social structure, J. abn. and soc. Psychol., 1962, 64, pp. 303–307.)

So, although not all errors in spelling are a function of serial position, it is certainly apparent that a large share are. It is difficult to suggest a practical application of this finding, although one is very likely to result. For instance, to facilitate learning to spell, one might print the middle part of words in *red* so as to emphasize them. This suggestion corresponds to the von Restorff procedure in serial learning in which one item in a series is set apart in a special manner. Sad to say, although the part set aside is learned more rapidly, what is gained here is lost through increased errors elsewhere. Performance on the list as a whole remains the same. In fact, in studies that have tried to reduce errors in spelling by just such emphasis of difficult parts, the von Restorff effect holds: No improvement in spelling of whole words even though performance with the emphasized part of the word is improved.

The von Restorff effect runs counter to the serial position effect. If the emphasized item is in the middle of a list it produces a pronounced drop in the very hump of the error curve. Clinton B. DeSoto and John J. Bosley suggest a persuasive interpretation of the serial position effect, one that also applies to the von Restorff effect. They had 28 college students, evenly divided according to class membership, learn to associate the labels "freshman," "sophomore," "junior," or "senior" with each of 16 names printed on cards. A subject had three seconds to supply the label and could then check the back of the card to see whether he had been right or wrong. *After each run-through of the deck of 16 cards, the experimenter shuffled the cards* and allowed the subject to begin again. There was no serial order in any trial. Yet in the error curve for the four labels, presented in order in Figure 4-7, notice the resemblance to the serial position curve. DeSoto and Bosley explain both their results and the serial position effect in terms of a subject's search for reference points around which he can build his learning. In a serial list of nonsense syllables the end positions serve as anchors; when there is no serial order a person will use the organization provided by the stimuli, such as class order. The von Restorff effect is another example of this search for a standard. Printing a nonsense syllable in a different color or a different size sets it up as the point of reference; consequently the learning of the rest of the list is built on the initial learning of this foundation.

Associations in Serial Learning

When we pointed out earlier that the probability of *G* as an association to *F* increased if *F* were preceded by *A B C D E,* we ascribed this increase to associations between each of these five letters and *G.* Such associations influence the errors made in the course of serial learning. Errors in list learning are typically of two major types: (1) Either a subject says nothing when asked to anticipate the next word, or (2) he says a word out of sequence. Depending on the direction of the mistake, it is called an *anticipatory error* or a *backward error.* Anticipatory errors far exceed backward errors in number. The occurrence of both types supports the notion that there are multiple associations among all words in a serial list. Thus, words appearing early may serve as partial stimuli for words appearing later in the list.

A more direct manner for assessing these connections is to use an association procedure. In this procedure subjects first learn a list of nonsense syllables or words. At the end of training, they are presented with each of the items in the original list, and asked to say the first word each suggests. Most subjects tend to give the next word in the series as their first association. A few subjects give the item two places later, and fewer subjects give a word more than two places away. Figure 4-8 shows how many subjects in an experiment

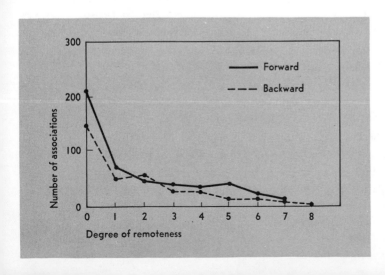

Figure 4-8. Number of forward and backward associations as a function of the remoteness between two nonsense syllables in a serial list. (From J.A. McGeoch, Amer. J. Psychol., 1936, 48, 221–245.)

of this sort gave an association at each position in the list. Note that associations are less numerous in the backward than in the forward direction; few associations are more remote than three steps away.

To sum up: (1) Connections exist between all items in a series. (2) These connections are stronger in the forward than the backward direction. (3) These connections tend to affect serial learning by appearing as anticipatory and backward errors. In order to learn the total serial behavior these tendencies must be overcome.

Rudolph W. Schulz has suggested that the more remote associations that plague learners may be the result of generalizing context cues. One cue for a response in a serial list is the position of the item in the list. Subjects often report that they remember that the *second* nonsense syllable is JIK. We know that generalization along positional dimensions is common. The context cue for position number 2 in a list is similar to that for position number 3. Because of the similarity of positions 2 and 3 the context cues for one might elicit the response for the other. Schulz has provided evidence supporting this interpretation.

THE LEARNING OF CONCEPTS

When a child first learns to say the word "doggie," he usually applies it to horses, cows, and cats. Bit by bit, after many corrections and reinforcements, he may begin to restrict his usage to dogs he regularly encounters. Even though he may wonder about chihuahuas and wolves, he is learning a type of category-naming called *concept formation*. The child's trouble with limits reflects the fact that the arbitrary categories we establish are matters of convenience. Nature is usually arranged in continua that spill over the end points of our concepts.

What determines the ease of developing concepts? Edna Heidbreder hypothesized that it depends on the kind of concept involved. Thus, concepts that represent concrete objects (trees, faces, hats) should be learned more easily than more abstract concepts (such as threeness or justice) that cannot have a single objective referent. To test her idea, Heidbreder asked subjects to learn the concept names of the pictures in Figure 4-9. She confirmed her hypothesis—subjects learned to assign a name to the different kinds of *faces* before they learned to respond with a name to the various pictures containing *three* objects.

H.D. Baum, however, challenged Heidbreder's interpretation. In repeating Heidbreder's experiment he noted that subjects frequently experienced confusion between instances or examples belonging to different concepts. The

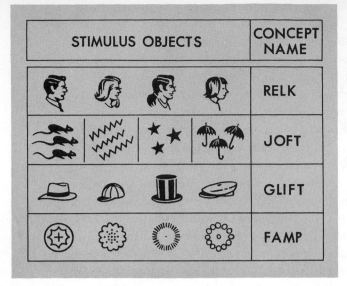

STIMULUS OBJECTS	CONCEPT NAME
	RELK
	JOFT
	GLIFT
	FAMP

Figure 4-9. Types of stimuli used by Heidbreder in her study of the development of concepts. Notice that although each of the stimuli differs from the others, the four stimuli that carry a common name have a basis of similarity. (From E. Heidbreder, J. gener. Psychol., 1946, 24, 93–128. Adapted by D.D. Wickens and D.R. Meyer, Psychology, rev. ed. New York: Holt, 1961, p. 362.)

most confusion occurred with instances that could elicit competing concept names. Thus, if twoness were represented by two faces, subjects often responded with the name appropriate to "faceness." Abstract concepts are almost always represented by instances that have many other competing concepts embedded in them. This is not so true of instances of concrete concepts like trees. These competing responses make concept learning a complex habit and are the chief reason that a child finds it more difficult to learn a concept than a conditioned response. Consider the number of potential competing responses when a child is learning to acquire the response "building" to both a shack and a skyscraper.

This analysis in terms of competing responses suggests that if we knew all the associative responses an individual had to each of a group of stimuli, we would be well on the way to being able to predict what concepts he would grasp from these stimuli. Since we would know of any competing responses to the stimuli we could also predict the ease or difficulty he would experience. Benton J. Underwood has proposed a theory of concept formation that is relevant here. He suggests that learning or recognizing concepts requires that one see relationships among stimuli. He hypothesizes that in order to see such a relationship it is necessary that the same associative response occur to each member of a group of stimuli. For example, if a child sees a blue triangle and a blue square he must have the association "blue" to both stimuli before he can see the relationship and form that concept. In order for a child to understand that a group of animals are *dogs* he must have learned to label them appropriately and the response "dog" must occur to each member of the group. Underwood also requires that these associative responses occur in temporal

p. 63 Learning — background

p. 298 Ed. Psych "

p. 211 Learning + human — "
abilities

contiguity; the greater the temporal contiguity the less difficult the formation of the concept.

In order to make it possible to conduct research along these lines, Benton J. Underwood and Jack Richardson prepared a set of verbal materials. They asked undergraduates to associate to each of a large group of words. The notion was that if they could get a number of words with a common associate (for instance, atom, crumb, flea and gnat all elicit the associate "small"), these could be used in the study of concept formation. They quickly discovered that free-association responses were too scattered and could not be usefully grouped. They then restricted their subjects to *sense impression* associates including such things as colors, shapes, sizes, textures, weights, smells, sounds and so forth, and in this way they found sufficient agreement for their research purposes. Thus, in the example given above, "small" was the sensory associate to gnat in 76% of the cases, to crumb in 79% of the cases, to flea in 86% of the cases, and to atom in 87% of the cases. To the word "eye," 32% responded with "round," 26% with blue, 10% with small, 8% with brown, and 6% with shiny.

A good deal of research has been completed using these materials. As might be predicted it has been found that the greater the average probability of the stimulus-concept association in a group of stimuli, the faster the concept is attained. Take the four words

Baseball   Head   Button   Knob

What sensory-impression concept do they represent? No doubt you very quickly came up with "round." You might have also noticed "hard." But you were most likely to come up with round first because as a sensory associate to these four words it has an average probability of 66.25%. Hard has an associative probability of only 8.25%.

If we take another group of four words, however, we can reverse the situation. Take

Knuckle   Hailstone   Skull   Stone

What sensory-impression concept do these four suggest? In this case "hard" is your most likely response (average associative probability of 52.5%); "round" is considerably less likely with an average associative probability of 11.25%.

Underwood and Richardson have shown that the probability of the concept-association is an extremely powerful variable determining ease of concept attainment. In these terms we can now look back at the Heidbreder instances in Figure 4-9 and understand better the relative difficulty in attaining the abstract concept. The association threeness is not a highly likely association to the picture of three mice; the association hat, though, is an extremely dominant one to a picture of a hat.

A pianist playing a piano, a tennis player smashing an ace, an adult reading a book, and a telegrapher sending a coded message are all examples of highly skilled serial behavior. How can we characterize the learning of such skilled performance? First of all, we must realize that an adult, or child, generally comes to a skill-learning situation with a wide variety of habits already available to him. These habits may be quite complex or relatively simple. For example, when learning to swim, a person knows how to kick, to move his arms around, to breathe in and out, before he actually goes into the water. These are all examples of relatively well-established serial behavior. They run off smoothly and without a hitch. Actual instruction begins when a teacher demonstrates the appropriate *integration* of these acts. For example, our neophyte swimmer knows how to move his head and how to breathe, but in order to use the breast stroke successfully, he must practice combining head movements and breathing. Combining these separate acts takes some time. But eventually the entire breathing and head-moving sequence runs off smoothly and becomes a single unit rather than a combination of separate units. Next, kicking and arm strokes must also be integrated with the breathing sequence. When a person has become highly skilled in the breast stroke the total serial behavior runs off (1) without faltering and (2) without forced conscious awareness of the component units.

A landmark in the study of skill learning was completed by William L. Bryan and Noble Harter in 1899. They examined the way telegraph operators learned to send and receive Morse Code. What they found parallels what we just said about swimming. At first, the student telegraphers learn the sounds (in receiving) and finger movements (in sending) associated with each of the letters. The student telegrapher receives and transmits messages letter by letter. With practice, certain frequent words (that is, series of letters) become quite familiar, and the telegrapher is able to send and receive these as *words,* rather than as a sequence of letters. He has moved from the letter-habit to the word-habit stage. Even as the telegraph operator is learning how to send and receive some words, he is also beginning to learn to recognize common phrases. What seems to emerge from research in skill learning is this: It is not so much that a person gets faster and faster with the small units, rather that he combines more and more of these small units into a single smooth unit so that more is accomplished in "one stroke."

Typing provides another illustration of the combining of units. To a new typist the sequence of letters T, H, and E are just that: a sequence of three letters. To the somewhat more experienced typist, T, H, and E are the word THE, which she types at almost a single stroke. For her the sequence forms a more complex unitary response. Similarly, a highly skilled secretary probably considers the phrase: "In reply to your letter of the . . ." as a single complex response. She is able to type it without faltering. The way the various components combine in typing may be presented as follows:

Early—Letter habit: I-n-r-e-p-l-y-t-o-y-o-u-r-l-e-t-t-e-r
Middle—Word habit: In-reply-to-your-letter
Final—Sequence habit: inreplytoyourletter

There are many variables that will affect the speed of skill learning. One of the most effective of these is *knowledge of results,* especially when it is specific and immediate. The effect is reminiscent of rewards in operant conditioning. In World War II Fred S. Keller was charged with the responsibility of devising improved methods of radio operator training. By providing conditions for immediate reinforcement of correct responses, Keller dropped the failure rate in the school to a fifth and cut the hours of training to two-thirds the former level. One important feature of this training program that should be mentioned is that the trainees enjoyed it. Their enjoyment helped maintain their motivation at an appropriate level for the task.

Do skills continually improve, or do they reach a stable level? In everyday life it would seem that we do reach a stable upper limit, probably because we rarely have any clear indication of how well we are doing, and because we are satisfied with a relatively adequate performance. With championship athletes or artistic performers, however, the story is quite different. It is rare for peak performance in either of these areas to be reached after just a few short years of intensive practice. When performance does level off it is probably due to aging. Instances of improvement in performance over a long period of time are hard to come by in laboratory situations, however. There is, though, some scattered data on the effects of continued practice in highly skilled performance in industrial settings. In one analysis, an investigator examined the number of cigars produced by a piece-work employee over the course of seven years. The results indicated that even after seven years' practice, the cigarmaker still continued to improve his performance. Thus, in skill learning the uppermost limit of capacity is a rare exception rather than a general rule.

These increases in performance at the higher levels seem to depend a good deal on the interest of the performer. The cigar-maker and the champion athlete increase their skill because they are interested in their performance whether for financial or personal reasons. Higher levels of skill are not reached by repetitious, half-hearted performance. Monotonous repetition, in fact, does not increase skill; it seems only to make lower-level performance more automatic. Here is another instance of how motivational factors shape the course of learning. Chapter 5 explores this influence in detail.

Complex
Habits

Motivation
and Learning

In Chapter 1 we introduced the notions of motivation a) as an energizer, b) as a stimulus, and c) as a need that can be satisfied. Now we shall discuss these three aspects of motivation again in greater detail.

—

Primary Drive

Within reasonable limits, increases in motivation lead to increases in activity A human infant when hungry stops sleeping and begins to kick and cry. A female rat in a period of high sexual

68

5

receptivity will run about nine miles a day in a squirrel cage; after being spayed, she will run less than a mile a day. You can intuitively understand the dramatic motivating effect of an electric shock, as described in the introductory chapter. These types of physiological motives (hunger, sex, and pain) are usually referred to as *drives,* specifically, *primary drives* because they seem to be built into the constitution of the organism, not learned as is a motive like the desire for sport cars. Like learning, such motivation is not directly observable. Here again, operational definitions help us in precise communication, since in any specific experiment we can define the level of a primary drive such as hunger in terms of the number of hours of food deprivation, or the amount of effort an organism is willing to endure in order to gain satisfaction. As an example of the latter, a rat, deprived of food or sexual activity, may be required to cross an electrically charged grid to reach an appropriate goal object. The level of shock he is willing to endure gives us some measure of the strength of the drive.

The strengths of drives have also been assessed by the resultant level of activity. In order to explore the effect of a primary drive on activity level W.T. Heron and B.F. Skinner starved some rats for many days, testing them daily during the course of the starvation. Before beginning the starvation program, they trained the rats to press a bar in a Skinner Box to obtain food pellets, and permitted the rats to eat their fill. Then, their daily diet was restricted to the food pellets they got as a result of four minutes of bar-pressing in the Skinner Box. This amount of food was too little to sustain life. Each day, following the four-minute period, the food delivery mechanism was shut off and the rats remained in the box for an additional hour. The increasing effect of hunger was assessed by the daily changes in the number of responses made during this hour. This measure reached a peak on the fifth day and then decreased rapidly as the rats began to suffer the physically debilitating effects of starvation. It seems clear that up to a point, responsiveness increases with increases in primary drive.

Although at the present time we can only guess what this relationship would be if it were not contaminated by the effects of weakness, there is a simple experiment that might determine this relationship. It would be an adaptation of an old experiment by Tschukitschew, who found that when he transfused blood from very hungry dogs into very well-fed dogs, the well-fed dogs began to act hungry. So it might be possible to starve rats to varying degrees and then to test how many Skinner Box responses well-fed rats would give after receiving transfusions from the differentially starved rats. Of course, the point would be that the transfused, well-fed rats would be "hungry" but their performance would not be affected by weakness.

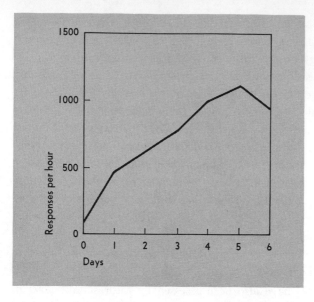

Figure 5-1.   Change in the mean number of responses per hour made by 13 rats during six days of food deprivation. (From W.T. Heron and B.F. Skinner, Psychol. Rec., 1937, 1, 51–60.)

Irrelevant Drives

We have seen how we can define the degree of hunger drive in terms of the conditions that produce it, of what the organism will endure to satisfy it, and of the resultant increase in activity level. In the last two categories the drive is clearly relevant to the measured behavior; that is, hungry rats get food for pressing the bar in the Skinner Box. Clark Hull suggested that all drives influencing an organism combine in their effect even if they are irrelevant to current behavior. This hypothesis stimulated a number of studies in which hungry rats were trained to run a maze for a food reward and then had the response extinguished while they were thirsty but not hungry. The control group was identical, except for being sated for food and water during extinction. In several such studies it was found that the thirsty rats took longer to extinguish the maze-running response, a result that seemingly supported the Hull hypothesis. But an instructive experimental error negated this support; it seems that when rats are very thirsty they don't eat very much, especially if the food they are offered is dry purina. Therefore, the rats that presumably were only thirsty were actually also quite hungry. As a consequence, they were under much higher hunger drive than the experimenter realized, which is why it took them longer to extinguish their response. Subsequent research has made it clear that irrelevant drives do not actively energize behavior in a learning situation. (We shall see, however, that anxiety as an irrelevant drive in people does produce some energizing effect.)

Does the level of drive
have an effect on learning as on performance? To explore this question experimentally we must train subjects under different levels of drive (say, one hour and 22 hours of hunger) and then test to see whether *learning* differences have resulted. One difficulty is that during testing the subject *must* be under some level of hunger. If he is fully fed before testing (zero hunger), then the *test* condition will be more like the one-hour than the 22-hour *training* condition. A decrement in response might result for the animals trained under 22 hours of food deprivation simply because of the change in internal stimuli. Testing under 22 hours of food deprivation would be unfair to the one-hour group.

A study by Donald J. Lewis and John W. Cotton made use of a special research design to overcome this problem. Two groups of rats were trained to run in a straight alley maze under one and 22 hours of drive respectively. The next day, one-half of *each* group was tested after one hour of food deprivation and the other half after 22 hours. Testing consisted of seeing how many trials it took to extinguish the running response. Presumably if it took longer to extinguish, it must have been a more thoroughly learned habit. The results are presented in Table 5. The numbers in the table report the average number of trials it took to extinguish the running response.

TABLE 5

Number of Trials to Extinction as a Function of Hours of Deprivation in Acquisition and Extinction

| | | Hours of Deprivation in Extinction | | Total |
		1	*22*	*Total*
Hours of Deprivation	*1*	90	117	207
in Acquisition	*22*	85	135	220
	Total	175	252	427

Note in this table the totals of the rows (207 and 220), and the totals of the columns (175 and 252). Each column total is contributed to equally by groups *trained* under one and 22 hours of deprivation. Therefore, the effect of the training drive is equal for the two *column* totals. If the column totals are different they reflect performance differences brought about by the two drives during extinction. As we might expect, the higher drive (22 hours) during extinction resulted in more responses before extinction was complete. Similarly, although the *row* totals are influenced by the drive during *extinction,* both row totals are *equally* influenced. Drive during extinction then could not produce a difference in the two row totals. The only antecedent condition that might produce such a difference is the drive during training. If drive during training did produce a difference in behavior during extinction, this would be the kind of relatively permanent change in behavior we ascribe to learning. In this experiment the row totals do differ. The higher drive for the 22-hour group during the learning period resulted in the formation of a maze-running habit whose extinction was prolonged. The effect is small but it is there. The same effect has been observed in other studies; even though it has not shown up in some studies, the sum total of evidence points toward the conclusion that learning under higher drive does lead to somewhat greater resistance to extinction.

But before we jump to the conclusion that we *learn better* under higher drive, let us examine a persuasive interpretation of this result. The effect of higher drive has been observed only in maze learning. Experimenters have observed that during learning, the high-drive group seems to be more strongly oriented to leaving the starting box than the low-drive group. Once learning has begun, the high-drive group traverses the maze in quite a business-like way while the low-drive group is a bit more meandering and exploratory. Actually both groups may be learning equally well, but they learn different habits. When extinction testing comes, the quick exit from the starting box and the business-like traversing of the maze on the part of the high drive group produces a combination that is more durable in terms of the particular requirements imposed by the experimenter. These considerations suggest that differences in drive are more likely to produce qualitative changes in learning than quantative changes in learning. That is, animals learn slightly different responses, rather than different degrees of the same response. These proposals also teach us that when we restrict ourselves to evaluating performance against so rigid a yard-stick as number of trials to extinction, we run the risk of losing important insights into the processes we are studying.

Interaction of Drive and Learning

In Chapter 1 we saw what happened when a rat, well educated in a T-maze, had eaten his fill—he slept. As we pointed out, this shows that *performance* depends on both motivation and learning. Clark Hull has proposed that their interaction must be multiplicative, not merely additive. That is, to determine what behavior will result in any given situation, we must multiply the drive level of the organism by the level of learning that he has achieved. (This can be achieved by converting both into arbitrary units.) If either is at the zero level we will get no responses. This hypothesis is quite useful in predicting behavior under different levels of drive. It has recently gained in importance since anxiety has been viewed as an energizing drive. Thus, we may use this hypothesis to predict the relative performance of persons with high and low anxiety on simple and complex tasks. But before we consider this proposal further, let us first see why anxiety may be considered a drive.

A Learned Drive: Fear

Criteria for the Existence of a Drive State.   We have shown how rats learn to fear a buzzer and how Albert learned to fear a rat. About the most reliable demonstration experiment in psychology consists of the conditioning of fear. If we use a distinctive CS and a strong electric shock, we can almost always obtain conditioning of a fear response in two or three trials. Fear is generally classed as an emotion. In addition, it meets the criteria for drives. What are they?

1. *Drives increase the activity of the organism.* Recall the Heron and Skinner starvation study and the sexually aroused female rats in the squirrel cage.
2. *Drives can motivate new learning.* A hungry rat will learn to traverse a rather complex maze to get to a food-laden goal box. When he is not hungry he may fall asleep in the starting box.

In a carefully planned series of studies, Neal Miller demonstrated that anxiety could be considered a drive in terms of these two criteria. (The words anxiety and fear will be used interchangeably.) He placed rats in a box with two compartments, one white with a grid floor, and the other black. The rats were at first indifferent to this treatment. Their indifference was modified by shocking them ten times in the white compartment. Each time they were allowed to escape into the black compartment. Later, when placed in the white compartment without shock they ran quickly into the black one, thus demonstrating that their activity was increased by their fear response to the cues of the white compartment. Fear, then, satisfies the first criterion of a drive state. But the second criterion, new learning, is not proved, since mere increased activity or a previously learned running response could have been operative.

In order to demonstrate that the acquired anxiety could motivate *new* learning, Miller altered the box by closing the door between the white compartment and the black compartment. Now the rats could only escape from the white compartment by turning a drum that opened the door. When

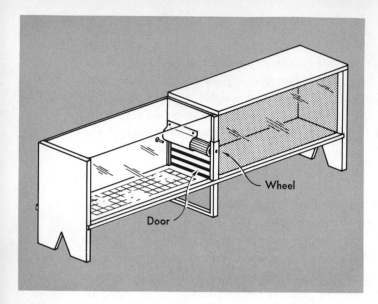

Figure 5-2. Apparatus used to train fear. Compartment A is painted white, compartment B, black. Electric shocks may be given in compartment A. Under different conditions the door (painted with black and white stripes) may be removed, and a low hurdle put in its place. (Adapted from N.E. Miller, "Learnable drives and rewards," in S.S. Stevens (ed.), Handbook of experimental psychology. *New York: Wiley, 1951.)*

placed back in the white compartment the rats manifested the usual signs of extreme anxiety—urination, defecation, and crouching. Eventually, they moved about and accidentally turned the drum; when the door opened they could run into the black compartment. Their speed in manipulating the drum and running into the black compartment increased rapidly with further such trials, thus indicating that the rats had indeed learned a new response.

Next, Miller more clearly established the potency of learned anxiety as a drive by making the drum inoperative and substituting a lever-press to open the door. The rats soon extinguished the drum-turning response and learned to press the lever. Both of these developments occurred without any additional electric shocks. The anxiety learned to the cues in the white compartment motivated activity (just as hunger might motivate activity) and the escape into the black compartment was a reward to the newly learned response (just as food might have been if the rat had been hungry). It seems clear that in terms of our criteria learned anxiety is a drive.

Fear-avoidant Responses and Their Extinction.

As a drive, fear energizes behavior. Miller's rats, driven by fear, ran to the black compartment to avoid a shock. When a rat reached the safety of the black compartment its fear was reduced, and this reduction reinforced the shock-avoidant response. Such learned fear responses and successful fear-avoidance responses are *extremely* resistant to extinction, as the following example shows. Richard L. Solomon has trained dogs to avoid a severe electric shock by jumping a shoulder-high hurdle separating two compartments. Ten seconds after the dog lands in the "safe" compartment he must jump back into the first compartment to avoid another shock. The same thing recurs in the first compartment, so the dog soon learns to spend all his time leaping back and forth between compartments. Figure 5-3 shows some interesting features of the dog's behavior in learning to avoid shock.

The important thing to keep in mind in studying this figure is that if the animal takes longer than ten seconds to respond it will get a shock. In this case the dog received only seven electric shocks, avoiding further jolts by jumping. By the twentieth trial the experimenter had turned off the electricity completely. Nevertheless the response continued to occur. Some dogs that have just been left to jump have continued to leap hundreds of times. Virtually the only way to extinguish the response is to prevent it by putting a ceiling on the box. After a desperate period of extreme fear the dog eventually calms down and does not jump even when the ceiling is removed. Any hint of shock, though, will set him off again.

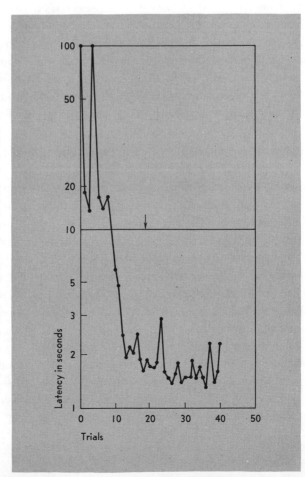

Figure 5-3. The performance record of one dog learning to avoid shock. The dog was shocked if he took longer than ten seconds to respond. The 10-second point is indicated by the horizontal line. All responses above this line (trials 1-7) were shocked. All responses below the line (trial 8 on) enabled the animal to escape the shock. The arrow indicates the point at which shock was permanently turned off. (From R.L. Solomon and L.C. Wynne, Psychol. Monogr., 1953, Vol. 67, No. 354, p. 6.)

Why is this response so resistant to extinction? If we stop reinforcing salivation to a CS it will soon stop; if the food is not in the goal box at the end of the maze the rat soon stops running. The crucial difference may be that in this instance of avoidance conditioning some reinforcement continues even after the experimenter has stopped administering electric shocks. As the end of the ten-second period draws near the dog begins to experience fear; when he leaps into the other compartment his fear is reduced, thus providing a reinforcement. Each time the avoidance response occurs, then, there is some reinforcement. One argument against this interpretation, however, is that after a dog has been in the apparatus for some time he usually performs his jumps every 1.5 seconds, yet the measurable latency of most fear responses (measured by indices such as GSR, heart rate change, blood pressure change) is greater than 1.5 seconds. So if the fear response has not yet occurred, how can the jumping response reduce it? The answer might be that there are components of fear that precede the *measurable* components. Perhaps these early components are the ones that are reduced.

Many theorists have explained neurotic symptoms as responses that fend off anxiety. Such symptoms keep a person from thinking anxiety-producing thoughts or serve to postpone or avoid anxiety-producing stimulation. For example, in obsessional neuroses individuals complain about persistent ideas that run through their minds and dominate their thinking. These thoughts may successfully insulate the individual from other, more distressing ideas. Relevant to this, it is difficult to treat some neurotic symptoms, about as difficult, perhaps, as extinguishing some anxiety-avoidant habits.

Anxiety in Human Beings. The most common way of defining human anxiety is in terms of scores on personality questionnaires, the best-known and most heavily used of which is Janet A. Taylor's *Manifest Anxiety Scale*. In this test, a subject is asked to say "yes" or "no" to such questions as "I worry more than other people" and "I blush easily." These are statements chosen by clinical psychologists and psychiatrists as being indicative of anxiety states. Taylor made the assumption that high scores on this test indicate high anxiety, which in turn indicates high drive. On the basis of Hull's formulation of the multiplicative interaction of learning and drive in determining performance, Taylor predicted that highly anxious individuals would be more susceptible to conditioning because of the effect of the higher drive. (Notice that in this case anxiety is an irrelevant drive.) A considerable amount of research has indicated that high scorers on the Manifest Anxiety Scale do indeed show more effective conditioning. As you can see in Figure 5-4 highly anxious individuals begin exhibiting more vigorous eyelid conditioning early in the conditioning session and widen the difference by the end of the period.

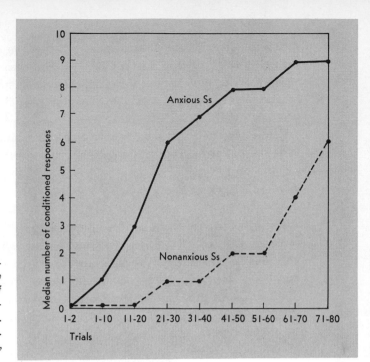

Figure 5-4. The effects of high and low anxiety on the speed of learning a classically conditioned eyelid response. (From J.A. Taylor, J. exp. Psychol., 1951, 41, 81–92, p. 88.)

In classical conditioning, often only one response is measured, or in some cases permitted. If drive increases, it energizes that one response, so more conditioned responses result. When we move to more complex learning, the picture becomes correspondingly more complex. A learning situation is complex, when, for one thing, many responses other than a correct one are possible. In addition, since it is a matter of *learning,* the correct response would not be the most likely one. If it were, there would be little to learn. Anxiety as a drive energizes all the habits that are evoked in the situation, incorrect as well as correct. Consequently, in a complex situation in which a weak tendency to respond correctly must compete with stronger tendencies to respond incorrectly, high anxiety, by multiplying the strength of both tendencies, should increase the absolute difference between them to the detriment of the correct response. For an arbitrary example, if at one drive level the correct response has two units of strength and the incorrect response has five units of strength, the absolute difference would be three units in favor of the incorrect response. If we double the drive level, the response strengths also double, becoming four and ten. The absolute difference in favor of the incorrect response is now six units. The deduction following from this relationship is that highly anxious persons would perform worse than less anxious ones in complex learning situations. Research has provided fairly consistent support for this deduction.

There is one difficulty here, however. When the experimental procedures do not threaten the subjects no difference has been found between individuals with different degrees of anxiety. The greatest differences have been found where some threat has existed in the situation. This suggests that a high score on the Anxiety Scale indicates a *readiness* to experience anxiety in appropriate circumstances rather than a chronic condition. The anxious person does not appear to "carry his anxiety around with him."

A Learned Hunger Drive?

Although learned fear is easily demonstrated, there has been great difficulty in providing unequivocal evidence that positive drives such as hunger which motivate approach responses can be learned. The difficulty may lie in the exclusive use of animals. We know for sure that human beings have many learned positive drives. They will work hard and learn many new responses to acquire prestige and wealth, neither of which directly satisfy primary drives. But about animals we are not certain.

Still there has been some success in attempts to condition this sort of drive in animals. Chimpanzees will go to some trouble to acquire wealth in the form of poker chips they can use in slot machines that dispense grapes. Although they work faster and better if the earnings can be immediately converted into grapes, the chimpanzees are able to postpone gratification, even completing fairly complex tasks before claiming their primary reward. They will also accept the poker chips as rewards for learning other, more complex, problems.

In an experiment paralleling Miller's research on learned fear, an attempt was made to train "hunger." Essentially, Miller had provoked fear in his rats while they were in the white compartment. For a three-week period James S. Calvin, Elizabeth Bicknell, and David S. Sperling placed rats in a striped box while they were hungry. Control rats were placed in the striped box when they were satiated. When both groups were then fed in the striped box, the experimental group ate more food. Apparently, they had learned to respond to stripes with hunger. We have a good idea that learned fear involves physiological activities associated with arousal of the autonomic nervous system. What physiological concomitants are there for learned hunger? Perhaps it would have been useful to have measured stomach contractions in this experiment. (While it has been difficult to replicate this finding, it has been described for its heuristic value.)

It is clearly more difficult to arrange conditions to teach hunger than it is to teach fear. Miller has suggested that the sudden onset of fear makes it easy to associate with a specific external stimulus. Hunger takes a while to develop;

you cannot turn it on suddenly. Consequently, it is difficult to pair in a neat fashion with an external stimulus.

As we have just demonstrated, drives have energizing properties. Further, as we pointed out in Chapter 1, associated with these drives are characteristic stimulus patterns. Operationally, it is difficult to distinguish between the conditions necessary to produce the energizing properties and the stimulus properties of drive. In the case of hunger, food deprivation does both. Then why make the distinction? For one thing, by using an independent measure of response such as activity in a squirrel cage, or rate of bar pressing as a standard, we can "equate" two drives, say hunger and thirst, for their energizing properties. We know, however, that the stimuli growing from stomach contractions and dryness in the throat would be different. If these are distinctive stimuli in the usual sense, it should be possible to train different responses to each. Clark Hull and Robert Leeper conducted early experiments demonstrating this possibility. They deprived rats of food on some days and water on other days. On foodless days the rats had to turn *right* in the maze to get food; on waterless days, they had to turn *left* to reach water. The only means they had of determining which direction to turn were their internal drive stimuli. It turned out that rats were quite successful in learning to respond correctly to their internal states.

Afterwards, though, it was argued that a discrimination between drive stimuli had not necessarily been established, for on thirst days the rats were given as much food as they would eat just before the test trials. Could it have been that the rats only learned to respond to an empty versus a full stomach? Subsequent research, however, studying only the drive stimuli of hunger, showed that rats could learn to turn left or right depending on whether they were experiencing drive stimuli resulting from 11.5 hours or 47.5 hours of deprivation. In both of these groups the rats were running on completely empty stomachs but they were able to respond in accordance with their drive state. It seems clear that drives have distinctive stimuli associated with them and that responses may be learned to these stimuli.

In Chapter 2 we introduced *contiguity theory* through the work of W.J. Brogden. This theory maintains that only one condition is necessary for learning—the co-occurrence of a stimulus and a response. The *law of effect,* or reinforcement theory, recognizes the necessity of contiguity but insists that it is insufficient—reinforcement is also necessary. Reinforcements can take an alarming variety of forms. Olds and Milner reinforced by electrical brain stimulation; Salzinger and Pisoni reinforced by social approval. What is the nature of a process that can apply to both of these disparate phenomena?

The Nature of Reinforcement

Clark Hull saw motivation and reinforcement as being related to the Darwinian theory of natural selection. As he portrayed these phenomena, they have survival value for an organism. Thus, it is useful for an animal to become active after missing a meal since this will increase his likelihood of discovering one. If his partaking of this meal (reinforcement) increases the likelihood of the acts that made it possible, then the probability of the continued existence of the animal and, consequently, the species is enhanced. In this system, motivation functions to increase the tension level of the organism; reinforcement leaves its mark by *reducing this tension level.* Food reduces the tension related to hunger; water does the same for thirst; copulation reduces sexual tension; pain is reduced by its termination or lessening; learned fear is reduced by removal of the appropriate stimuli. One problem in this explanation is that the reinforcement acts backward in time, affecting the probability of a response that preceded it. This is illogical; an effect cannot precede a cause. Hull recognized this difficulty and suggested that a response is followed by a neurophysiological process called a *trace,* which "represents" the response in the nervous system. It is this trace that is reinforced. But how is tension-reduction involved in the stimulation of the brain? Perhaps what Olds and Milner discovered is the center in the brain where tension-reduction is registered. Direct internal stimulation then would have the same effect as external need-reduction.

According to this theory we should always be seeking and hovering around situations that are associated with tension-reduction. The success of rollercoasters and horror movies is a rather uncomfortable fact that this theory has not fully explained. Attempts at explanation always recall the story of the man who loved to be beaten because it felt so good when it stopped. Despite this and other faults, however, tension-reduction remains the one explanation of reinforcement that accounts for most of the data and observations. It seems likely that the next development in this area will come from the laboratories of those psychologists studying the neurophysiology of learning.

In summary, tension-reduction is currently the explanation of the nature of reinforcement that explains most of the data. As is generally true of the development of science it will not be discarded because of some contrary evidence. It will be replaced when a better explanation is available, most likely a neurophysiological one.

So much for the nature of the reinforcement effect. What is the status of reinforcement in current psychological theory? Demonstrations that learning can occur without reinforcement, such as that of Brogden's, are not uncommon in the literature. Such evidence eventually caused Hull to place more emphasis on the role of reward in motivating behavior. Hull was the chief exponent of the law of effect in the second quarter of this century. His shift in emphasis in his theoretical orientation reflects that of most learning researchers, who now generally view reinforcement as being extremely important in performance, but as exercising little direct effect on learning. Through its role in determining performance, however, reinforcement retains a crucial role in learning.

THE NEED FOR CHANGE AND REST

To this point we have discussed motives that are satisfied by the organism's increasing its activity. There is also a class of motives that can best be satisfied by a cessation or change of activity.

The Need for Stimulus Change

At McGill University 22 male college students were given $20 for every 24 hours they would spend lying in a soundproof room on a foam rubber bed, wearing translucent goggles, gloves, cardboard cuffs around their arms, and a U-shaped foam rubber pillow for their heads (see Figure 5-5). Nothing was required of them; in five days, though, they could earn $100. Yet, few of them were able to stand the job more than two or three days. The students found it exceptionally difficult to sleep or think; they had hallucinations and became panicky; and they dealt poorly with intelligence tests introduced during their stay in the room. When they emerged from the experiment they were often disoriented, confused, nauseous, and fatigued for periods up to 24 hours. While some of this effect is due to the suggestibility of the subjects, the root of this disorder of behavior is lack of satisfaction of a need for stimulus change.

Perhaps the capacity to be bored is one of man's important qualities, though we share this capacity with lower animals. Rats and monkeys, at least, have shown a need for changing stimulation which can motivate new learning. In one experiment Robert A. Butler and Harry F. Harlow showed that non-hungry monkeys would learn to differentiate between panels of different

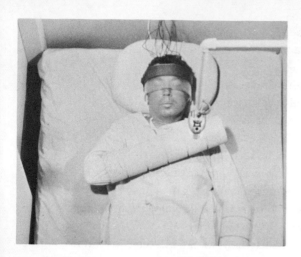

Figure 5-5. Typical experimental arrangement used in sensory deprivation studies. (From Gateways to the Mind, Bell System Science Series *film.)*

colors with no other reward than the opportunity to look out a window into a different room. When a monkey pushed a panel door of one color the panel opened and he was permitted to look through into another area for 30 seconds. When he pushed the other-colored panel it did not open. Monkeys learn to discriminate between colors on the basis of this type of reward alone.

In another experiment rats were trained to distinguish between the white and black arms of a T-maze. The only reward for a correct choice was the opportunity to explore a more interesting maze for one minute. The mean number of correct choices in the T-maze showed a significant increase as the number of trials increased. Rats chose the site that provided the greater stimulus change.

The results of all these experiments indicate that both men and animals respond favorably to changes in stimulus. Indeed, this desire for a change in stimulus conditions is strong enough to induce the learning of new responses that will bring changes about. If "boringness" of a stimulus condition leads to a tendency to get away from that condition, then the effectiveness of novelty in evoking new behavior should diminish as an animal becomes more familiar with a new situation. In support of this supposition, a number of studies have shown that although rats tend to explore new objects, this tendency diminishes as the animals become more familiar with the objects. Due to stimulus generalization, other objects similar to the now-familiar ones will also be ignored. This result is perfectly congruent with the others we have mentioned and would suggest that the slogan "It's time for a change" applies equally well to stimulus conditions and to politicians.

The Need for Cessation or Change of Activity

Animals seek stimulus change; research on response boredom tends to emphasize fatigue or the need for rest as the critical factor. From some rather ingenious demonstrations by Kurt Lewin and his coworkers, however, we know that fatigue as an explanation may not always be completely accurate. In one study, for example, a subject was instructed to copy a given figure repeatedly. After a short time he complained that he was tired and could no longer continue drawing. Thereupon, the experimenter asked him to write out a description of what he felt and thought about the task. Without hesitation the subject picked up the pencil, wrote out his description and even included a drawing of the figure he had just said he could no longer reproduce because he was so tired. Clearly, there is more to response boredom than simple fatigue. But this does not deny that boredom develops; its importance to learning cannot be overestimated. We are all sorry witnesses to the necessity of repetition in learning material of any degree of complexity. Learning would be greatly facilitated if the effects of response boredom could be reduced. Let us now turn to an examination of the various ways repetition or practice may be arranged in order to facilitate the learning of new materials.

Following the notion that fatigue is instrumental in response boredom, investigators have arranged the learning of materials so as to test the effects of rest, during which fatigue could dissipate. Carl Hovland interpolated rests between items in a list of 12 nonsense syllables and also interpolated rests between trials on the total list—either two seconds or four seconds between items, and either six seconds or 126 seconds between lists. There were four different groups.

Group 1 had two seconds between nonsense syllables and six seconds between lists.

Group 2 had two seconds between nonsense syllables and two minutes and six seconds between lists.

Group 3 had four seconds between nonsense syllables and six seconds between lists.

Group 4 had four seconds between nonsense syllables and two minutes and six seconds between lists.

The results of this study are shown in Figure 5-6. The two top curves show the results for groups 1 and 2 (item interval of two seconds); the bottom two curves present the data for groups 3 and 4 (item interval of four seconds). The results indicate that greater spacing, both between items and between separate repetitions, produce fewer errors and better learning. The effect of spacing is greater, however, between items than between trials. That is, a very small amount of rest between individual items in a series more than compensates for a relatively large amount of rest between complete trials of the whole series. Interitem rest probably allows for dissipation of response fatigue. *Distributed or spaced practice* produces better learning of serial lists than does *massed practice*. This is true for both spacing between items and

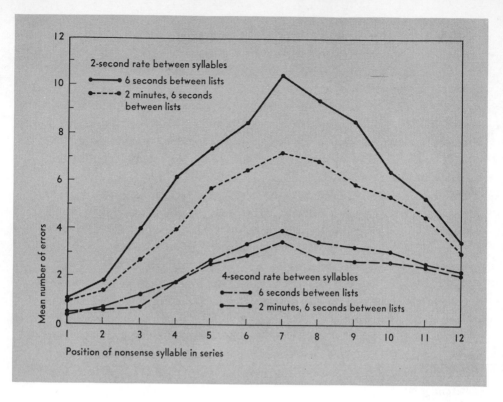

Figure 5-6. Effects of interitem and interlist rest periods on the serial position effect. Note: In this figure the ordinate of the graph counts the number of errors, so that a high score indicates a poorer performance than a low score. (From C.I. Hovland, J. exp. Psychol., 1938, 23, p. 178.)

spacing between lists. (Similar findings have also been reported for rats learning serial mazes.)

Does the efficacy of spaced practice apply to all types of learning tasks? The answer is, *mainly*, yes. Not only does distributed practice help in the learning of serial lists of nonsense syllables, but it also facilitates the learning of motor tasks such as sawing wood, driving a car, knitting, and bicycle riding. In fact, this effect is *greater* for motor tasks than for serial lists.

Psychologists have studied motor learning with an apparatus called a *pursuit rotor*. Figure 5-7 shows a simple example of this type of equipment. Here a subject's task is to keep the stylus (A) in contact with the circular target (B), which is set near the edge of the revolving table. Doing so completes a circuit that runs an electric clock. The subject's score is his time on target. In one experiment by Gregory A. Kimble and Robert Shatel, two groups of college students were each tested for ten consecutive days. Each

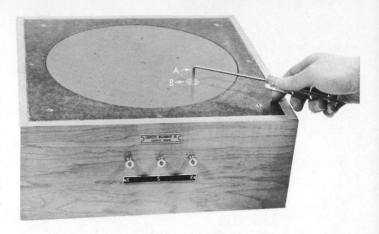

Figure 5-7. Rotary pursuit apparatus. The subject's task is to keep the stylus in contact with the circular metal target while the platform revolves continuously. (Photo courtesy Lafayette Inst. Co., Lafayette, Ind.)

day they had fifteen 50-second trials. In the massed practice condition there was a five to ten second rest between each trial; the spaced group had 65 to 70 seconds between trials. The results of this experiment are presented in Figure 5-8. For each of the ten days on the graph, the first, second, and last points present the actual figures for trials 1, 2, and 15. The third point represents the average value of trials 3 to 8; the fourth point represents trials 9 to 14. The percentage of time subjects were on the moving target in each 50-second

Figure 5-8. Effects of massed and distributed practice on motor learning. For explanation of the graph see text. (From G.A. Kimble and R.B. Shatel, J. exp. Psychol., 1952, 44, 355–359, p. 356.)

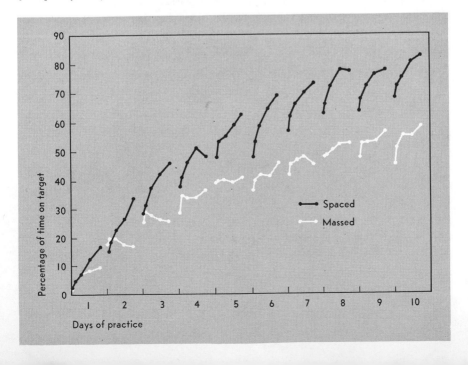

period is plotted on the ordinate of this graph. The figure reveals a number of results.

1. Clearly, *spaced* practice aided performance on the task; learning under spaced practice increased more quickly and reached a higher level at the end of ten days than learning under massed practice.

2. Note that both groups show a *marked* increase from trial 1 to trial 2 every day. This is known as the *warm-up effect*. This reflects the need, on beginning a task after a long rest, for some practice to get back in the groove.

3. After this initial spurt, continued practice in the massed practice group often results in a decline in performance. This decline is called the *work decrement*, or *reactive inhibition*, and is commonly associated with learning through massed practice of the same response.

4. Compare the second trial on days 2, 3, 4, and 5 with the last trial of the preceding day (we use the second trial and disregard the warm-up effect). Notice the marked improvement in performance that resulted from the rest, and without practice. This improvement, called *reminiscence*, represents recovery from the work decrement and also suggests the magnitude of the decrement. The lesser improvement in the spaced group corresponds with our expectation that they would suffer less build-up of work decrement.

5. Here again we see an instance of the need for the distinction between learning and performance. The declining performance after the warm-up effect for days 2, 3, 4, and 5, is actually a period of increasing learning. After the dissipation of the work decrement the effect of this learning shows itself.

6. There is, over and above the warm-up effect, forgetting, which takes place overnight. The longer the interval between practice sessions the greater the forgetting. The curves for days 2, 3, 4, and 5 for the massed group seem to show no forgetting (again discounting warm-up). This is because their performance is so badly retarded by the work decrement.

The advantages of spaced practice generally outweigh its disadvantages. Still, when the material to be learned is rather brief, and not inordinately difficult, massed practice has the advantage in that learning might be accomplished before much work decrement develops. Also, massed practice minimizes intertrial forgetting. There is one more exception: In paired associate learning massed and spaced practice do not differ if the response members of the pairs are distinct or quite familiar to the learner. Finally it must be stated that the greater efficiency of spaced practice is evident only when total *work* time is considered. If the time for rest intervals is taken into account massed practice is often *more* efficient. Spaced practice leads to effort efficiency; massed practice leads to temporal efficiency.

What can we conclude? In learning most tasks, it helps to insert regular rest intervals into practice as often as is practical. Such spacing is most beneficial with motor tasks. In fact in learning motor tasks, we can often gain *more* from a period of rest than from continued practice. When learning verbal material by rote, such as poetry or a speech or historical facts, frequent rest between items also increases efficiency. When we come to learning more complex tasks, spacing can still help us where the materials are unfamiliar. Thus, in learning vocabulary in a new language, or mastering a mathematical proof involving *unfamiliar* concepts and symbols, spacing of learning is useful. On the other hand, spacing of practice only wastes time where the responses to be learned are familiar but have to be given a new meaning or connected to a different stimulus. In mathematics, learning a variant of techniques using familiar operations and symbols, or in language learning, mastering a list of cognates, the tasks proceed as well with or without rest intervals.

In this section, we have brought together, *sensory deprivation,* and *work decrement,* both of which are variables that result from the monotonous repetition of stimulus or response conditions. We described the way each can influence learning and retention. *Sensory deprivation* seems to result in major disruptions in behavior and in a strong need for stimulus change. If stimulus change is given it provides a reinforcement that increases the probability of the preceding response. *Work decrement* (also called *reactive inhibition*) is a form of accumulated response fatigue that results from the repetition of responses during learning. *Spaced practice,* or the allowance of frequent rests, causes less work decrement than *massed practice* since it permits accumulated response fatigue to dissipate. Consequently, the learning of verbal and motor tasks is usually aided by spaced practice. Motor tasks benefit more, perhaps because they result in greater accumulation of response fatigue. Massed practice is more efficient in short learning tasks and in cases of learning a new organization of very familiar material.

Transfer of Training

New York City is dotted with playgrounds that provide outdoor handball courts. As in tennis, boundary lines mark the playing area in these courts; the focus of a court is a front wall against which players propel a ball, using a motion best described as a slap. The players are free to step anywhere, but the ball must only touch down within the confines of the boundary lines. As I learned the game in daily play, it was a free and open sport requiring vigorous running. The reason that this blatant nostalgia is relevant to a discussion of transfer of training lies in what happened when I recently accepted

88

6

a handball challenge from a graduate student. Because of my earlier extensive practice in outdoor handball I was sure that I would more than hold my own, even though we would be playing indoor, or four-wall, handball. Now, four-wall handball is played in a windowless room and the focus of play is again the front wall, against which the ball must eventually be propelled. As you might imagine, my previous training in one-wall handball transferred quite effectively as long as the volley was confined to midcourt away from the unfamiliar side and back walls; this sort of help from previous training we call *positive transfer*. I soon discovered, however, that before or after hitting the front wall the ball might legitimately bounce off any other wall. Being a bit of a slave to my previous training, I was frequently lunging to the left to meet the ball, which was busily hitting the left wall and bouncing off to the right. Such interference from previous training is called *negative transfer*.

WHAT TRANSFER IS

We can draw a few insights from the handball incident. For one thing, maximum positive transfer results when a new task is extremely similar to one already learned, as in straightforward midcourt play. When the new task is only somewhat similar, then considerable interference, or negative transfer may develop. Since the old handball experience would not directly influence my current chess game, we might also guess that when past and present tasks are for all practical purposes completely dissimilar, then the effect is neither positive nor negative but simply neutral. Figure 6-1 presents these generalizations diagrammatically.

This diagram is helpful in describing transfer in a general way. Yet, when we get down to cases, we soon find some questions that this model cannot answer. For example, how do we measure the similarity between old and current tasks? Do we concentrate on the responses made in the two situations or on the stimuli? In this chapter we shall examine transfer in relation to stimuli, to responses, and to the interaction between them. Before attacking these problems, though, we shall describe some of the research techniques used in this area.

Laboratory Procedures Used to Measure Transfer

If you stop to think about it for a minute, it is quite remarkable that while looking in a mirror a woman can put on lipstick or straighten her hat, or that a man can shave or straighten his tie. Right and left and front and back are completely mixed up in the glass. Learning is obviously necessary in order for a person to per-

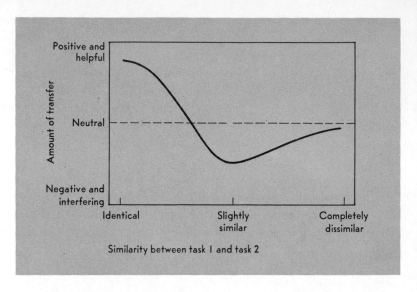

Figure 6-1.   Effects of task similarity on transfer. Where task 1 and task 2 are identical or very highly similar, performance on task 2 is facilitated; where they are only slightly similar, performance on task 2 is hindered; where they are completely dissimilar, performance on task 2 is unaffected. (Adapted from E.S. Robinson, Amer. J. Psychol., 1927, 39, 297–312, p. 299.)

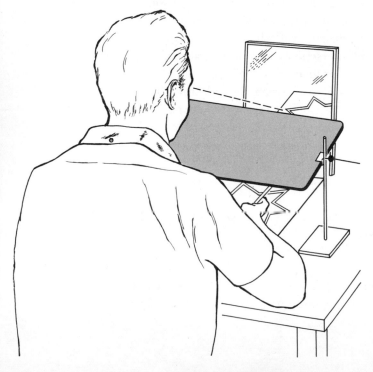

Figure 6-2.   Schematic diagram of a mirror-tracing apparatus. The subject sits facing the star, which is visible to him only in the mirror.

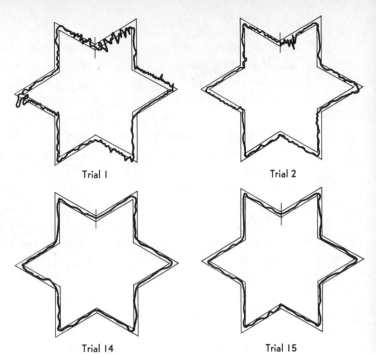

Trial 1

Trial 2

Figure 6-3. Changes in mirror-tracing performance as a consequence of practice. (From H.L. Kingsley and R. Garry, The nature and conditions of learning 2nd ed. Englewood Cliffs, N.J.: Prentice-Hall, 1957, p. 304.)

Trial 14

Trial 15

form a movement that is directed solely by mirror cues. Psychologists, therefore, have been quite interested in the way mirror reversals are mastered.

The procedure most often used to study this type of learning is mirror tracing. A typical mirror tracing apparatus is shown in Figure 6-2. In this task a subject is required to trace the outline of a star with only a mirror's reflection to guide him. At first his experiences make it difficult for him to move his pencil in the correct direction. Subjects have remarked that the pencil seems to stick to the edge of the outline as if the outline were magnetized. This "magnetism" is, of course, nothing more than the subject's own push in the wrong direction. With practice, however, he becomes able to fill in the star quite easily. Figure 6-3 shows an actual record of the stages one person went through in learning to master this task. Notice that on the early trials a tremendous conflict in response is evident in the large number of little movements around each part of the star where a change in direction is necessary. As learning progresses, these conflicts become less and less evident in the record. If sufficient practice is afforded to a subject, all interfering movements disappear. This is precisely what is happening in the case of a woman putting on her lipstick or of a man shaving while looking in the mirror.

The conflict in the early stages of mirror drawing is largely the result of *prior* left-right and front-back training. For adults, earlier habits are the major source of interference in learning a new task. But later experience can produce interference too, in this case with the performance of earlier learning. Suppose we have a rat learn one maze, then learn a second maze, and finally test his performance on the first maze again. We would expect that the rat would incorrectly use some habit related to the second maze in his retest on the first one. In fact, we *would* observe some such interference. This interference, contrary to our mirror-drawing example, is the result of an experience that *followed* rather than preceded the first test performance.

These two cases provide examples of the two major methods used to study transfer in the laboratory. Schematically, the first of these procedures runs as follows: Learn Task A (or assume A to be known) and then test on Task B. In order to determine the effect of the prior learning of Task A on Task B, it is necessary, of course, to include a control group with no experience on Task A. In the simplest version, a single experimental group and a single control group are used in the following way:

Experimental Group: Learn A   Test B

Control Group: Rest   Test B

This type of experimental model is called a *proactive transfer design* (from the Greek prefix *pro,* meaning before, hence transfer effects that are the result of previous activity). If Task A does have an effect on Task B, then the two groups should differ in their performances on Task B. If learning Task A helps to learn Task B then we say that *proactive facilitation,* or positive transfer, has taken place. If learning Task A depresses performance on Task B, then we say that *proactive interference,* or negative transfer, has occurred. If there is no difference between the two groups, clearly no transfer has taken place.

The second major type of experimental procedure used to study transfer has the following design:

Experimental Group: Learn A   Learn B   Test on A

Control Group: Learn A   Rest   Test on A

This pattern is called a *retroactive transfer design,* retroactive because Task B has a throwback effect on Task A. If the interpolated Task B actually does affect performance on Task A, then the two groups should differ in their test performances on Task A. If B helps in the performance of A, then *retroactive facilitation,* or positive transfer has taken place; if B is a hindrance, it is because of *retroactive interference,* or negative transfer.

The mirror drawing test is an example of a proactive design. A subject comes to this task already having learned how to follow visual cues in moving to the right or to the left. Experiences have provided previous training. Now he is asked to learn a new way of orienting his movements in a changed right-left and front-back perceptual field, so his prior orientation hinders his performance in learning a new response during early trials. Under these conditions he shows proactive interference.

Mirror drawing is also applicable in a retroactive transfer design. In one experiment of this type two groups of subjects are first given an opportunity to trace the outline of a star with their left hands (that is, the nonpreferred one). One group then gets to practice this task with their right hands (the preferred hand); the second group rests. Both groups then have a few more tries at tracing the pattern with their nonpreferred hand. The results of a great number of experiments show a *positive bilateral transfer effect;* that is, those who practice with the right hand perform better on subsequent trials with the left hand than those without practice. This experiment also presents evidence for retroactive facilitation. This facilitation probably consists of learning how to use cues from the mirror rather than of learning how to make specific movements.

Stimulus Factors in Transfer

In Chapter 3 we considered one type of transfer based on stimulus factors, *stimulus generalization.* Here, a response transfers positively from one situation to the next because of the similarity of the situations. When the same response is required in two such similar situations, the amount of positive transfer to be expected from the old situation, A, to the current situation, B, is shown in Figure 6-4. As you

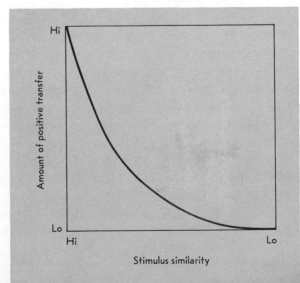

Figure 6-4.   A typical stimulus generalization gradient. As stimuli become more dissimilar, less positive transfer is expected.

can see, as the current stimulus situation becomes less and less similar to the old situation the amount of positive transfer decreases.

Let us examine an experiment by Kwang S. Yum that tested the relationships shown in Figure 6-4. Yum's subjects first had paired-associate training in which the stimuli were geometric shapes and the responses were nonsense syllables. The next day they were shown a list of geometric shapes and asked to respond with the correct nonsense syllable. Now, only some of these test shapes were the same as the ones they had seen the previous day. The remaining test shapes were of varying similarity to the original patterns. Yum wished to see whether the similarity would cause subjects to respond with the nonsense syllable paired with the original pattern. The results, presented in Table 6, show that the greater the similarity, the greater the recall of the nonsense syllable.

TABLE 6

An Example of Positive Transfer
as Related to Stimulus Similarity

Rated Similarity of Test Pattern to Original Geometric Pattern	Percentage of Subjects Responding With Original Nonsense Syllable
Least similar to original figure	36.32
More similar	45.30
Similar	49.15
Very similar	64.53
Identical to original figures	84.62

Note that even in the "least similar" category there was some positive transfer. When the response (in this case the nonsense syllable) is the same in the old and current situations, transfer is almost always positive and almost never negative. The amount of positive transfer depends on the similarity of the stimuli; the more the similarity the greater the positive transfer.

A more recent experiment examined the effect on transfer of a different sort of stimulus similarity. In this project each subject first learned a series of paired associates in which the stimulus was a meaningful word—for example, slow—corlep. In the second part of this experiment, for each of three different groups of subjects a different stimulus word was substituted for slow. They were fast, dim, and flaming. The response, corlep, however, remained the same for all three groups. Slow and fast are word associates—that is, if you show a subject the word slow, his first associate is most often fast. When studied by a complex rating procedure called the semantic differential, slow and dim belong together in terms of shared meanings. Fast and dim then are related to slow. Flaming, however, has little or nothing in common with slow; flaming—corlep essentially served as a control condition for evaluating the effect of the other two words in producing positive transfer.

The experiment clearly showed that it was easiest to learn a second pair if the second stimulus word was a direct associate to the original stimulus term (fast—corlep). Words with similar meaning (dim—corlep) showed somewhat less positive transfer. Unrelated words (flaming—corlep) showed little or no transfer.

These two experiments show that when a person is faced with a new situation in which he must learn to make a previously practiced response his previous experience will probably help him. The amount of help will depend on the similarity of the new to the old situation. There will be some positive transfer no matter what form the similarity takes.

Response Factors in Transfer

A respected rule of thumb in psychology is that when you move from one situation to another you will always get negative transfer if you keep stimuli constant but change the responses. A good example of this is a person who has learned to drive a car using a clutch and then switches to the same model car with automatic transmission. The stimuli are not terribly different but the responses have changed radically. This individual will find himself stabbing frantically with his left foot looking for the clutch and fumbling around with his right hand in the place where the gearshift should be. In the laboratory, learning XAD—PIV will be harder if you have previously learned XAD—GEJ. Let us first acknowledge the general applicability of this old rule and then turn to examine some of the exceptions. They help us to understand the more general rule better.

Here is one exception: W. N. Kellogg and Edward L. Walker trained a dog to lift his right hind leg to a combination of buzzer (CS) and shock (UCS). They next attempted to train the dog to lift his left hind leg in response to the buzzer. They found positive transfer, for the dog learned to lift his left hind leg more quickly than he would have without having previously learned to respond with his right hind leg. Note that in this experiment the original and subsequent response were compatible. That is, the dog was supported by a sling in the experimental apparatus; raising his left leg after the buzzer did not prevent him from raising his right leg. In this situation, positive transfer occurred because the old response was not incompatible with the new response, and both responses were highly similar. Only, in fact, when new and old responses are compatible and somewhat similar will positive transfer occur. As the similarity of the responses decreases, it very quickly increases the likelihood of negative transfer. Where the two responses are incompatible and dissimilar, negative transfer is greatest.

Another, more subtle example of how compatibility of responses can make positive transfer possible may be seen in a study by Jarvis Bastian. First he had subjects learn a list of syllable-word pairs, like XAD—dark. Then he divided them into three groups that were differentiated by substitutes for dark. The substitute responses were light, black, and calm. Bastian found that the substitution of the first two words produced marked positive transfer. The reasons are not difficult to find. First, the words light and black are closely related to the word dark. Indeed, exactly 829 of 1008 college students give light as their first association to dark. Second, the responses are not incompatible. Subjects can easily *think* the word dark between the stimulus and new response without interfering with their performance: thus,

$$XAD \rightarrow (DARK) \rightarrow LIGHT.$$

In these experiments we see exceptions to the general rule that when we replace a response with a new response, negative transfer results. When the two responses involved are compatible, positive transfer is possible. This clearly suggests that one reason for negative transfer when responses are replaced may be incompatibility, so that the old interferes with the new.

Summary

If we consider a task as consisting of a specific stimulus and response pair $(S_1—R_1)$, then it is possible to examine what happens as we vary one or both of these components. If we hold both the stimulus and response items constant we expect maximum positive transfer. In this condition we are only giving our subject one more learning trial. If we hold the response term constant but vary our stimulus term, we expect some positive transfer, the exact amount depending on the similarity between S_1 and S_2. If we hold the stimulus term constant but vary the response, we expect negative transfer in most cases. The only case in which we would expect some slight positive transfer is where R_1 and R_2 are not incompatible. Although we can exercise some control over stimuli and responses in the laboratory, it is difficult to find situations in which only the stimuli vary or only the responses change. A baseball player learning golf, a one-wall handballer learning four-wall handball, a college student learning his second foreign language provide examples of transfer situations that defy simple analysis in terms of either stimulus or response. In most such cases where we vary *both* the stimulus and the response terms, we expect some negative transfer.

We all know individuals who can take difficult puzzles and tricky problems and solve them in a fraction of the time most of the rest of us could. Much of their facility is doubtless due to their being attracted to such pastimes and consequently having practiced many puzzles before. But their facility extends even to puzzles where the stimuli and responses could not bear any direct relationship to puzzles they have seen before. Here we have a situation of positive transfer where both stimulus and response factors have changed. Often such positive transfer can be ascribed to learning how to learn, that is, learning a mode of attack.

Probably the best evidence for learning how to learn comes from a series of experiments done by Harry F. Harlow and his associates at the University of Wisconsin. In these experiments they presented a monkey with a series of discrimination tests each using two blocks. For each test these two blocks were clearly different in terms of some easily perceivable cue—one white, the other black; one cylindrical, the other conical; one striped, another plain; and so on. The monkey was allowed to look under only one block on each trial in a test series. Each time, some reward, such as a raisin, was in a well under one of these blocks. If, on his first test trial, the monkey lifted the white block and did not find the raisin, he would be using optimal strategy if on the second trial he looked under the black block. For the first few tests with different pairs of blocks, the monkey did no better than chance on both the first and second trials. As the monkey gained more experience in the test series, his second guess in any specific test series became consistently better. In fact, after most monkeys had done about 200 different cue-discrimination tasks, they chose the correct block about 90 per cent of the time on the second trial. With 300 discrimination problems mastered, the monkeys were 95 per cent correct on their second trials.

The monkeys seemed to learn general habits, in response to the total test situation. For one thing, they learned which aspects were crucial and which irrelevant. For example, they learned not to respond to the position of the block, but to the pattern on it. Finally, they learned to *switch*. If the prize was not under the first pattern selected, they did not try that pattern again. If we had only had the opportunity to observe these monkeys being tested on their 300th problem, we might have been tempted to ascribe their performance to "insight." Knowing their previous experience, however, gives us an understanding of their current ability. It also suggests the role of learning how to learn in our daily lives. We continually encounter new situations to which

Transfer
of Training

97

we must respond adaptively. These new situations are usually similar in form to things we have experienced before. Learning to learn efficiently enables us to evidence what we call insight, rather than random trial-and-error behavior. It is instructive to note that lower animals do not evince much learning to learn, not even cats or the low-order primate marmoset.

Similar results have been found with rats running mazes and human beings learning lists of nonsense syllables. In both cases it takes longer to learn the first maze in a series or the first list in a series, than it does to learn subsequent ones. Figure 6-5 shows the number of trials subjects needed to learn lists of 12 nonsense syllables as a function of the number of previous lists they had learned. Clearly, fewer trials are required to learn later lists than to learn earlier lists. Learning how to learn is involved here also. If a memory drum is being used, subjects must learn the rhythm of the device. In paired-associate learning individuals often attempt to bridge the pairs with a mediating word. Nonsense syllables are examined for their resemblance to real words. In addition, many irrelevant responses drop out. A person's emotional response to a new test situation subsides; noises go unnoticed; room stimuli that are not relevant are disregarded. What goes into learning how to learn is such a pot-pourri of acts which are specific to each new situation that it is difficult to state general principles. We can, however, stress the importance of making an early determination of the *essential* stimuli and disregarding the irrelevant aspects of the learning situation.

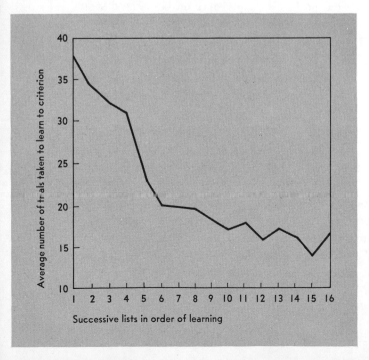

Figure 6-5. Curve demonstrating "learning to learn" with verbal materials. Note that nearly every succeeding list is learned in fewer trials than those that preceded it. (From L.B. Ward, Psychol. Monogr., 1937, Vol. 49, No. 220, p. 13.)

By way of summary, then, we may say that positive and negative transfer are the results of carrying over both specific components and general modes of attack from one task to another. In talking about specific components as the basis of transfer, we generally analyze an old and a current task into their respective stimulus and response components. If stimuli are varied and the response common to both tasks is kept constant, then positive transfer results. The degree of similarity between stimuli and two tasks determines the amount of positive transfer. If stimuli are kept constant and responses are varied, then negative transfer results in most cases. Positive transfer occurs only insofar as the second response is compatible with and highly similar to the first response.

Remembering
and Forgetting

For several weeks as part of an experiment on memory, a psychologist named Harold E. Burtt spiced his two-year-old son's daily reading-time diet of Mother Goose and Winnie-the-Pooh with three selections from Sophocles. What was particularly remarkable was that he read these selections in the original Greek. The son's reaction to this regimen was not reported. Six years later, however, Burtt tested for possible remnants of the passages in the child's memory. Without explanation, he asked his now eight-year-old son to memorize these same three selections and three equivalent Greek

7

selections that the boy had never seen or heard. Burtt reasoned that if the boy learned the old selections more quickly, the exposure six years earlier may have had some effect in facilitating the later learning. Indeed, Burtt found that it took 435 repetitions for his son to learn the new selections but only 317 to learn the old. This case provides rather striking anecdotal evidence for the persistence of the effects of learning.

In this chapter we shall be concerned with whatever influences our ability to retain material we have learned. It is clear that understanding memory is central to understanding learning. Obviously, there could be no improvement from trial to trial if a learner did not remember something from preceding trials. He builds on what he remembers from previous experience. We call the hypothetical residue left by previous experience a *habit*, a *bond*, or a *memory trace*.

A second reason for our concern with memory in a book on learning is that we are interested in the fate of learned behavior over various time periods. The study of memory allows us to examine changes in learned behavior that are uncontaminated by further practice.

Before we begin this study let us examine the three basic methods psychologists use to measure memory in the laboratory:

1. Recall.
2. Recognition.
3. Relearning.

The first and second of these methods are quite familiar to all students. An essay examination is an example of a recall test. *Recall* requires a person to tell what he has learned by producing the correct responses. A multiple choice question, on the other hand, is an example of a recognition measure. *Recognition* is a matter of discriminating what one has learned from other materials, a matter of identification. As any student can tell, recall is far more difficult than recognition. *Relearning* is a measure of retention not usually used in classroom tests. In order to get at this measure we ask a subject to learn something, say, a list of nonsense syllables. He then gets a rest period, which may vary in time from a few seconds to a few years. Next we ask him to relearn the initial material. If there is a decrease in the time required, in the number of errors made, or in the trials needed to relearn the list, then we have some indication of the persistence of memory. Relearn-

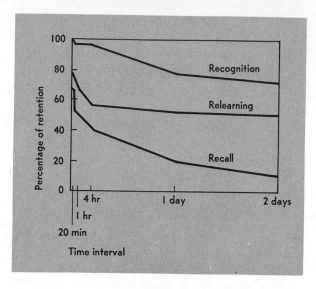

Figure 7-1. *Differences in the amount retained as a function of the method of measurement. (Adapted from C.W. Luh,* Psychol. Monogr., *1922, 31, No. 142.)*

ing is a sensitive measure and will usually show the effect of memory even in cases where the other two measures do not detect any retention at all. Burtt's boy *relearned* the three Greek selections in 317 repetitions, whereas it took him 435 repetitions to learn similar new material. His earlier experience with the material was helpful, an effect that could only be detected by the relearning procedure. If asked to recall or to recognize the previously learned material, the boy almost certainly would have been unable to do so.

The three methods vary in sensitivity. Fig. 7-1 shows the effect of this variation over an extended time period. Recall, inevitably, produces the lowest scores. While in this figure recognition yields the highest retention scores, these scores could easily be lowered by embedding the to-be-recognized items in highly similar material. A nonsense syllable is easier to recognize in a group of colors than among similar syllables. This does not mean that a memory trace is stronger when we test through relearning or recognition. It is just easier to detect the persistence of memory when we use a more sensitive measure.

THE NATURE OF FORGETTING

We have twice referred to memory as a "trace." Psychologists are not yet in a position to state what the nature of this trace is, however, nor where in the nervous system it is deposited. Nevertheless, it seems reasonable to hypothesize that somehow events are recorded in order to explain their later recall. Some psychologists have ascribed *forgetting* to the gradual fading of this hypothetical trace through disuse. They reason that if the trace were heavily used the memory would be retained. However intuitively appealing this notion may be, it is generally contradicted by research evidence. We know from our discussion of classical conditioning that the best way to cause "forgetting" (or extinction) of a conditioned response is to evoke it repeatedly in the absence of the unconditioned stimulus. Repetition in and of itself does not prevent forgetting; nor is forgetting primarily a consequence of disuse.

Two Explanations of Forgetting

What then is forgetting?

We shall discuss two important current explanations of this phenomenon. The first grows from previous research on perception, which has provided evidence that our remembrance of what we have seen tends to change in specific ways. It is hypothesized that all memory changes in these same ways, and that it is these alterations that produce the forgetting. For example, if

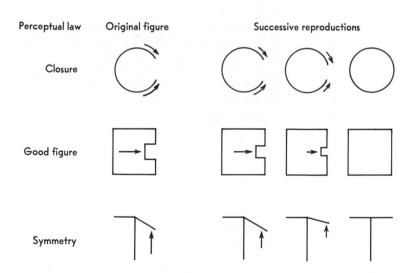

Figure 7-2.   Progressive changes in memory traces predicted by the perceptual laws. Direction of predicted change is indicated in each case by an arrow. (From C.E. Osgood, Method and theory in experimental psychology. *New York: Oxford University Press, 1953.)*

a subject is shown any of the original figures in Figure 7-2, his memory of them will shift to the more symmetrical and less imperfect figures shown in the column on the far right. Each change is brought about by a different special principle. The three principles of change depicted in Figure 7-2 are:

closure (the tendency to close an open figure), *good figure* (the tendency to perfect a figure), and *symmetry* (the tendency towards a balanced figure). These three principles are seen as physiological processes that are built-in aspects of the functioning of brain tissue. According to this view, because of these processes the trace laid down by experience becomes a more perfect and better balanced figure, and thereby loses some of its own characteristic qualities. This change in the trace, then, is the cause of the forgetting of the original figure. If a trace is particularly asymmetrical the eventual formation may have only little relation to the original material, and considerable forgetting may be a direct result.

A second explanation of forgetting ascribes it to the tendency of habits to interfere with one another. How does this work? For example, in an experiment in verbal learning, a subject learns, say, the paired associate, "table—WEG." After a week he returns for memory testing. During the week he has seen many tables and made many overt and covert verbal responses to "table." According to interference theory, these competing responses crowd out the nonsense syllable "WEG" and cause forgetting. If the subject had not had any postexperimental interfering experiences a large share of forgetting would be avoided.

Probably the most famous study of interference was reported by J.G. Jenkins and Karl M. Dallenbach in 1924. They had two students learn a number of lists of nonsense syllables. One of the students went to sleep immediately after learning; the other student carried on with his normal daytime activities. At the end of one-, two-, four-, and eight-hour periods, the students were asked to recall the material they had learned. The sleeping subject was awakened after each of these intervals, only one interval being tested in any one night. Table 7 shows the average percentage of syllables

TABLE 7

**Percentage of Syllables Forgotten
as a Function of Time and Consciousness**

Subject's Condition	*Time Elapsed*			
	1 hr.	*2 hrs.*	*4 hrs.*	*8 hrs.*
Awake	54	69	78	91
Asleep	30	46	45	44

forgotten after each of the four different time intervals. According to these percentages the sleeping subject forgot less than the waking subject at each period. Note, however, that he did not have perfect retention at any point.

That 46 per cent of the material was forgotten during the first two hours may be due to the amount of time he lay awake before falling asleep or to thoughts or dreams during sleep. From the second to the eighth hour there was no significant increase in forgetting for the sleeper. The awake subject, on the other hand, showed a progressive increase in forgetting as a consequence of performing regular daytime activities. As Jenkins and Dallenbach concluded: "Forgetting is not so much a matter of decay (due to disuse) as it is a matter of interference, inhibition or obliteration of the old by the new."

The Trace Hypothesis

Having briefly stated the nature of these explanations, let us examine some of the relevant research evidence. The earliest experiment on the changing-trace hypothesis pertained to memory of perceptual form. Subjects examined an asymmetrical form, such as the one which is shown to the left in Figure 7-3. Each subject was then asked to reproduce the form repeatedly. After each reproduction the experimenter would examine the newly drawn figure for changes. The series of drawings in Figure 7-3 shows a progressive trend toward a more symmetrical figure. In this case memory for perceptual form would seem to be changing in the direction predicted by the law of symmetry.

Stimulus figure   Successive reproductions

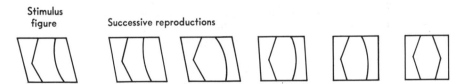

Figure 7-3.   Successive changes in the reproduction of a single stimulus figure by the same individual. (Adapted from F.T. Perkins, Amer. J. Psychol., 1935, 44, 473–490, p. 473.)

There is unfortunately one serious flaw in the conduct of these experiments: the same subject drew all the figures for a given series. It is entirely possible, therefore, that the original memory trace itself did not change in the direction of becoming more symmetrical, rather that the subject tended to use his memory of his own poorly drawn initial figure as the one to copy from, rather than the original stimulus figure itself. Yet, if the initial reproduction showed the predicted changes, is this really a valid criticism? Yes, because most of the figures used in these experiments did not have a single predictable direction of change. Therefore, it was difficult to evaluate the changes that occurred. Experimenters who were favorable to the trace change theory saw every alteration as evidence for a specific principle of change. Similarly, experimenters who were unsympathetic to this viewpoint saw every change as fortuitous, and not dependent on any specific principles. Thus, the interpretation of the experiment finally boiled down to a question of theoretical persuasion rather than experimental fact.

To correct this error, Donald O. Hebb and E.N. Foord used figures with clearly predictable patterns of change. Two different groups of subjects were shown a stimulus figure and then tested for recognition, one group after five minutes, the other after 24 hours. They did *not* have to draw a reproduction of this figure. *Recognition* was tested by showing the subjects a series of forms, all of which differed systematically from the initial stimulus form. Figure 7-4 shows one of these series. The original stimulus is labeled S.

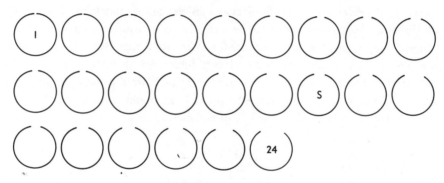

Figure 7-4.   Series of stimuli used to test for memory-trace change. Subjects were originally shown the stimulus labeled S. (Adapted from D.O. Hebb and E.N. Foord, J. exp. Psychol., 1945, 35, 335–348, p. 344.)

Mistakes in recognition could veer in one of two directions: (a) toward the best, most symmetrical form (the circle numbered 1), or (b) away from this best form (and toward circle 24). If the changing trace hypothesis is correct, then errors should tend toward circle 1 (principle of closure) rather than toward circle 24. Furthermore, there should be more such errors after 24 hours (during which the principle of change had sufficient time to be effective) than after five minutes. The results failed to reveal any such trend. Mistakes were not consistently in the direction of circle 1, nor were there more mistakes in this direction for the 24-hour group than for the 5-minute group. When careful experiments are performed, it seems that memory traces do not change in the direction predicted by perceptual laws of change.

Does this experiment rule out the possibility that *systematic* changes in memory occur? Certainly not. In a series of ingenious experiments, F.C. Bartlett had subjects reproduce stories and visual forms. He found that

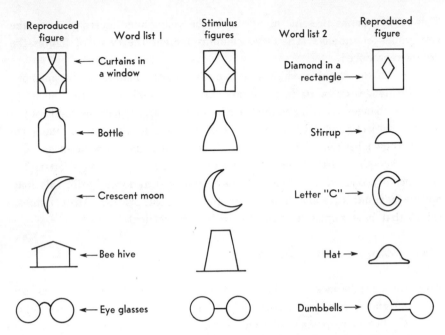

Reproduced figure	Word list 1	Stimulus figures	Word list 2	Reproduced figure
	← Curtains in a window		Diamond in a rectangle →	
	← Bottle		Stirrup →	
	← Crescent moon		Letter "C" →	
	← Bee hive		Hat →	
	← Eye glasses		Dumbbells →	

Figure 7-5. *Examples of how a verbal label affects the reproduction of an ambiguous figure. Subjects in one group were told that the first stimulus figure looked like "curtains in a window," while subjects in the second group were told it "looked like a diamond in a rectangle." Note the differences that appear in the figure reproduced by each group. (Adapted from L. Carmichael et al., J. exp. Psychol., 1932, 15, 73–86, p. 80.)*

changes in memory do take place, but that they are largely influenced by naming, or labeling. The general outline of the original material does not change as much as do details which are relevant to the labels the subject may give to a figure. If a subject sees an ambiguous figure as resembling some object familiar to him, his reproductions will gradually alter the original until it becomes the familiar object. The label he initially gives to the ambiguous figure shapes his reproductions and his "memory trace" of the figure. More direct evidence of the role of labeling comes from an experiment done by Leonard Carmichael, H. P. Hogan, and A. A. Walters. They presented subjects with a group of ambiguous figures, with instructions to draw them from memory after the entire group had been presented. Just before one of the experimenters exposed each figure, he told one group of subjects that the ambiguous figure looked like a familiar object and named the object. He showed the same figures to a second group of subjects and told them the figures looked like some other familiar object, again named. After going through an entire series of figures, the subjects were asked to draw the figures. The middle column of Figure 7-5 shows materials used in this experiment.

The outer columns present the names of the ambiguous figures given to the two groups of subjects. The outer columns present the types of figures the groups reproduced.

Many of the drawings show a strong effect of the naming of the memory traces. Changes do occur in the reproduction of visual forms from memory, but these changes, contrary to the trace hypothesis, are largely the result of the name a subject provides for the original stimulus. In the case of the form ⊤ , shown back in Figure 7-2, the reason it may be reproduced as ⊤ is that the subject has remembered it as "looking like the capital letter, T." Our memory does seem to move toward symmetrical forms. Still, this may not be a result of some innate neurophysiological process. Most familiar things that have names happen also to be symmetrical.

An Interference Analysis of Forgetting

Retroactive Interference.   The interference analysis of forgetting suggests that material is lost to memory only when it is displaced by some other material. The mere passage of time between initial learning and recall does not cause forgetting. Some process or event must interpose itself to produce forgetting. In line with this, psychologists have devoted a good deal of time and energy to investigating the effect of various ways of filling the time interval between original learning and the recall of learning. The retroactive transfer experiment described in the previous chapter is one technique that was devised for this purpose. Let us analyze this experiment in terms of interference theory.

As pointed out in the preceding chapter most often studies of retroactive interference have used the following three-stage procedure:

Stage 1: A paired associate task is presented to the subject. To make our discussion easier let us follow the fate of one pair, A—B.

Stage 2: An interpolated pair, with the same stimulus term, A, and a new response term, X, is presented to the subject for learning.

Stage 3: The subject is now asked to relearn the original pair A—B or to recall B in the presence of A.

If we examine this procedure carefully we can see that the subject has learned the pair A—B in Stage 1. In Stage 2 he must now respond with X. When this learning is complete the subject has learned the pair A—X. Stimulus A now tends to produce both B and X, thus, $A\diagstrut_{X}^{B}$. Response X then interferes with response B in Stage 3 when the A—B pair must be relearned. Forgetting of B may take place because response X is interfering.

Using a similar analysis, Arthur W. Melton and J.McQ. Irwin had five groups of subjects learn a list of nonsense syllables. This was *original learning* (Stage 1). One of these groups then rested before being asked to recall the original list. The second through fifth groups were asked to learn an interpolated list for 5, 10, 20, and 40 trials, respectively. This second learning constituted *interpolated learning* (Stage 2). At the end of interpolated learning all five groups were asked to recall the initial list (Stage 3).

As might be predicted from interference theory, the groups that learned interpolated lists tended to have more difficulty learning the original list. In general, the more the interpolated practice, the more the interference.

Proactive Interference.   This experiment makes it clear that one source of forgetting is the experience we have between the time we learn something and the time we try to remember it. But isn't there another possible source of interference in memory? What of all the experiences that precede what we have called original learning? This produces *proactive interference.* Many psychologists maintain that the chief cause of forgetting in adults is old habits.

The way one psychologist tracked down the pervasive effects of proactive interference on memory reads like a piece of master detective work. Benton J. Underwood noticed that in some laboratories subjects seemed to be able to recall as much as 80 per cent of the material they had learned, whereas in other laboratories subjects were only able to recall about 10 per cent. Ebbinghaus, who certainly was a master at recalling nonsense syllables, evidenced recall of only about 35 per cent of the material he had learned. Could it be that a college student who had learned only one list could remember nonsense syllables better than a great scientist who had learned literally hundreds of different lists? It seemed incredible. Underwood began his investigation by examining a number of preliminary questions:

1. Were there differences in the materials used in the different laboratories? By and large the answer was no.

2. Did procedures vary from laboratory to laboratory? Again the answer was generally no.

3. Did the subjects vary? Actually, the subjects did vary in terms of the amount of experience they had had in verbal learning experiments.

Underwood sensed that here was the chief clue. Accordingly, he went back to all the published experiments and carefully compared the treatment of experimental subjects. After extensive sorting of evidence Underwood discovered the key to the puzzle. Students in one experiment, who had learned 16 different lists before the time they were asked to recall the last list, recalled only about 20 per cent of the material they had learned. In a study in Underwood's laboratory, where each subject learned and recalled only one list, the recall rate was as high as 75 per cent. After examining the reports of results in 14 different experiments, Underwood concluded that the percentage of material subjects recall is clearly related to the number of previous lists they had learned (see Figure 7-6).

What this means is that interference in recall is dependent in large measure on a subject's activities and habits before a present task. Proactive interference, in the form of already existing habits, is probably the major cause of forgetting. The phenomenal ability of children to recall details of events long forgotten by their parents is doubtless due to their shorter lives and consequent lesser degree of proactive interference. On the day when children begin to lose that fantastic ability to recall such details, we know they are beginning to grow up.

Consideration of the implications of proactive interference brought Leo J. Postman and Underwood to another puzzle. The letter sequence CAT is memorized more easily than the letter sequence KJB. But CAT has many responses attached to it from previous experience; these old habits should proactively interfere with learning. Either interference theory was wrong in this case or there are other potent sources of proactive interference that are less obvious. The one that turned out to be important in this context was proactive *letter-sequence interference*. Through careful tabulation of "which letters tend to follow which letters" in English, it soon became clear that KJB provides difficulties because subjects have previously experienced O following K far more frequently than J. Consequently, at the time of recall, O proactively interferes with J as a letter to follow K.

We have identified two extra-experimental sources of interference that

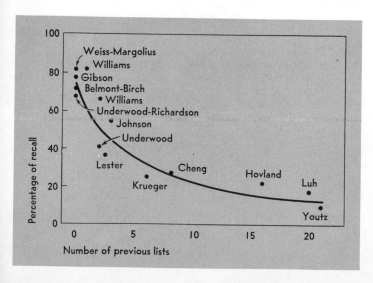

Figure 7-6. The effects of proactive interference on recall. Each dot represents the data obtained by a different investigator. (From B.J. Underwood, Psychol. Rev. 1957, 64, 49–60, p. 53.)

human beings bring to a laboratory memory situation: (1) interference from prior word association tendencies (cat-rat; black-white, and so on), and (2) interference due to past letter-sequence habits (CAT vs. KJB). These are both instances of the general rule that most material we learn must compete with pre-existing habits. This continual interference and "struggle for ascendancy" in our memory might be expected to result in a continuous jumble of thoughts. We are saved from this, however, by continually practicing important acts, such as dressing, finding our way to work, and conversing. Responses that are not practiced in this manner are likely to be replaced by new learning, or, in short, forgotten.

SHORT-TERM MEMORY

Up to this point we have discussed the attrition of memory over relatively long time intervals. It is also apparent that we often need to recall material over *short* time intervals. Remembering a telephone number, the name of the last few streets we passed in an unfamiliar town, or the preceding part of this long sentence are all examples of short-term memory.

Early experimenters studied the *memory span*. In the procedure used, a subject is read progressively longer sequences of numbers or letters. The length of the longest series he can immediately recall indicates the size of his memory span. Since this length may vary from trial to trial, we usually measure the span a number of times and express a person's span as an average score.

Is memory span about the same size for all kinds of material? According to one psychologist, the length of memory span generally equals the "number 7 plus or minus 2." What this phrase means is that an adult can normally remember 7 ± 2 items, whether these items are numbers, letters, nonsense syllables, or words. Regardless of the material, our short-term memory capacity remains about the same. This seems rather strange when we consider that whereas we can only recall 7 ± 2 letters, we can recall 7 ± 2 words even though the words probably have an average of five letters apiece, making a total of 35 letters in all.

What we seem to recall is not specific letters or numbers but *meaningful units*. George A. Miller has suggested that we recall "chunks" of information (that is, meaningful units) rather than the components of each chunk. The word "triskaidekaphobia" may exceed our memory span if we consider it as a series of 17 letters. But in this case, obviously, we recall not a number of letters, but one chunk of information. When Miller says that the approximate size of the memory span is 7 ± 2, he means 7 ± 2 *chunks*.

More recently Lloyd R. Peterson and Margaret Jean Peterson (1959) have developed a way of studying short-term memory that has yielded extremely surprising results. You would think that when presented with a single three-letter nonsense syllable, such as JIQ, an average college student would be capable of remembering it for nine seconds. As a matter of fact, he cannot! Peterson and Peterson presented students with such a single nonsense syllable and then asked for recall after either 3, 6, 9, 12, 15, or 18 seconds. Each student was only tested once. Since they wanted to minimize the possibility that subjects would rehearse the nonsense syllable, they asked them to fill the time between presentation and recall by counting backward by threes from, say, 66. Not more than 30 per cent of the students could recall JIQ after nine seconds had elapsed (see Figure 7-7).

In a series of similar experiments, Bennett B. Murdock, Jr., had subjects recall three different types of materials: nonsense syllables, common words, and a set of three unrelated words. He asked them to recall the stimuli after they had been exposed to the Peterson and Peterson technique—that is, KJB, 66, 63, 60 ....., recall KJB. The results for the three-letter nonsense syllable were similar to those reported by Peterson and Peterson. With the single English words, however, there was little or no forgetting over the entire 18-second recall interval. For the three unrelated words the subjects suffered a loss in memory comparable to that found for the nonsense syllables. Murdock's complete results are shown in Figure 7-8. Notice the similarity among Murdock's curves for nonsense syllables and three-word sequences and

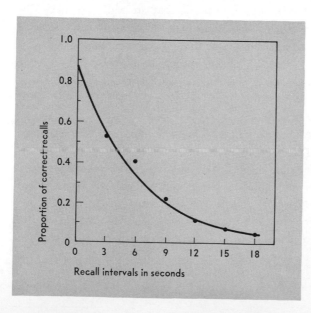

Figure 7-7. Short-term recall of three-letter nonsense syllables, using the Peterson and Peterson counting technique. This graph shows the proportion of correct recalls occurring with latencies of less than 2.8 seconds. Data points are actual; the curve has been fitted to these points. (From L.R. Peterson and M.J. Peterson, J. exp. Psychol., 1959, 58, 193–198, p. 195.)

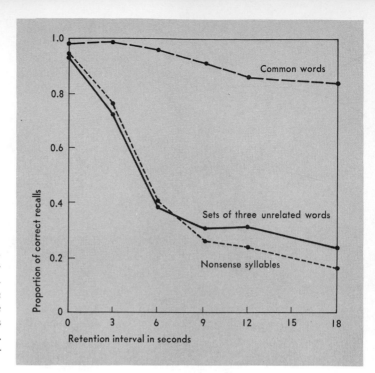

Figure 7-8. Comparison of the recall for three-letter nonsense syllables, simple English words, and sets of three common words. (From B.B. Murdock, J. exp. Psychol., 1961, 62, 618–625, p. 619.)

Peterson and Peterson's curve for nonsense syllables. This similarity again suggests that the span of short-term memory is determined by the number of chunks of information to be recalled.

Let us briefly summarize what we have found out about memory. In discussing memory we have concentrated on the other side of the same coin, forgetting. There is a theory that forgetting results from physiological changes in the brain which alter the original memory in certain lawful ways. Adequate research methodology has not supported this theory. Interference theory ascribes forgetting to the displacement of the originally learned material with other material. Retroactive interference is caused by new learning following the original material; proactive interference is caused by learning which preceded the original material. Proactive interference is the more important of the two in the lives of human adults. Finally short-term memory, we found, has a limited span, encompassing 7 ± 2 chunks of information for just about any form of material.

Selected Readings

Original sources

Guthrie, E. R. *The psychology of learning* (rev. ed.). New York: Harper, 1952.

Hull, C. L. *Principles of behavior*. New York: Appleton-Century-Crofts, 1943.

Hull, C. L. *A behavior system*. New Haven: Yale University Press, 1952.

Pavlov, I. P. *Conditioned reflexes* (Translated by G. V. Anrep). London: Oxford University Press, 1927.

Skinner, B. F. *The behavior of organisms: an experimental analysis*. New York: Appleton-Century, 1938.

Watson, J. B. *Behaviorism*. New York: Norton, 1925.

Interpretative statements and summaries

Hilgard, E. R. *Theories of learning*. New York: Appleton-Century-Crofts, 1948.
A straightforward and clear presentation of the major theoretical systems.

McGeoch, J. A. and A. L. Irion. *The psychology of human learning*. New York: Longmans Green, 1952.
A sound and thorough exposition of research in human learning.

Kimble, G. A. *Hilgard and Marquis' conditioning and learning*. New York: Appleton-Century-Crofts, 1961.
A complete and current presentation of the essential facts of learning with an especially good discussion of operant and classical conditioning.

Dollard, J. and N. E. Miller. *Personality and psychotherapy*. New York: McGraw-Hill, 1950.
An explanation of personality and personality disturbances in terms of Hull and Freud.

Skinner, B. F. *Walden two*. New York: Macmillan, 1948.
A description of a utopia built on Skinner's operant conditioning principles.

Index

McConnell, J. V., 2
McFann, H., 46
McGeoch, J. A., 6, 62
Meaning, conditioning of, 42
Meaningfulness of verbal units, 6–7, 19
Mediation:
    characteristics, 7–8
    in sensory preconditioning, 24
Mednick, S. A., 7
Melton, A. W., 109
Memory (*see also* Forgetting, Proactive
           inhibition, Remembering, Re-
           troactive inhibition, Short-term
           memory, Transfer):
    as affected by labels, 107–108
    as affected by schema, 106–107
    as a function of measurement, 102
    effect of number of prior lists learned,
        109–110
    methods of measurement, 101
    for perceptual form, 105–106
    role in learning, 101
Memory drum, 58–59
Memory span, 111
Memory trace, 102–103, 105–107
Miller, N. E., 35, 38, 73–74
Milner, P., 23
Mirror drawing, 91–92
Motivation (*see also* Drive, Reinforce-
           ment, Reward):
    as a cue, 9–10
    defining properties of, 8
    effect on activity, 69
    effect on learning, 8 ffg.
    as an energizer, 8, 68–79
    relationship to reinforcement, 79–81
    as a stimulus, 78
    as tension, 10–11
Murdock, B. B., 112, 113

N

Negative transfer, 89
Nonsense syllable:
    described, 6
    measurement of meaningfulness, 6
    reasons for use, 58

O

Olds, J. F., 23
Operant conditioning:
    comparison with classical conditioning,
        4, 52–53
    described, 3, 43–51
    summary of, 52
    use with mental patients, 3
Operant response, 43
Operational definitions:
    described, 20
    of motivational events, 69
Osgood, C. E., 103

P

Paired-associates learning, 7
Partial reinforcement (*see also* Reinforce-
           ment, Reward):
    defined, 45
    effects, 46–49
Pavlov, I., 3, 12, 27–30, 33, 37, 38, 39
Performance (*see* Drive, Learning, Moti-
           vation)
Perkins, F. T., 105
Peterson, L. R., 112, 113
Peterson, M. J., 112, 113
Pisoni, S., 43
Planarian, conditioning of, 1–2
Positive transfer, 89
Postman, L. J., 109
Primary drive (*see also* Drive, Motiva-
           tion):
    effects of, 68–69
Proactive interference:
    described, 109
    and/or facilitation, 92
Proactive transfer design, 92
Problem solving:
    Köhler's view, 11–12
    role of past experience, 12
    Thorndike's view, 11
Proprioceptive stimuli, role in mediation,
    24–25
Psychic secretion, 28
Psychogalvanic skin response (PGR), 20
Pursuit rotor apparatus, 84

R

Rate of response, 22
Rayner, R., 32, 37
Readiness:
    defined, 48
    relationship to shaping, 49
Recall, 101
Recognition, 101
Reflex, 27
Reinforcement (*see also* Drive, Motiva-
           tion, Reward):
    defined, 10
    exceptions to need-reduction hypothe-
        sis, 80–81
    intravenous, 11
    need-reduction hypothesis, 10–11, 80–
        81
Reinforcer, 43
    schedules of, 45–46
Relearning, 101–102
Releasing stimulus, 17
Remembering (*see* Forgetting, Memory)
Reminiscence, 86
Response:
    measures of, 21
    problems in definition, 20–23